EILEEN DIAMOND

LET'S MAKE MUSIC FUN!

THE RED SONGBOOK

Introduction

In this volume of **Let's Make Music Fun!** Eileen Diamond has included a colourful selection of familiar and new songs including action songs, part songs, story songs, instrumental songs and rounds, to form a unique library of topical source material suitable for pre-school, Key Stage one and Key Stage two.

Each song is provided with teaching ideas and notes on performance which help to explore and satisfy a whole range of National Curriculum requirements.

To help find the material you require, all the songs have been identified by Key Stage and song type. Piano accompaniments have been simplified and chord symbols have been added.

Children will enjoy singing these catchy songs over and over again. Fun to learn and fun to teach!

Music and text processed by Halstan & Co. Ltd., Amersham, Bucks., England

Cover Design by Paul Clark Designs

Published 1997

Contents

Alphabetical Song Listing

Learning A Round

Each round should be learnt in unison before part singing is attempted.The instrumentation listed for the rounds is only a suggestion and may be varied according to which instruments are available and the time. Although melody instruments are not used in these arrangements, there is no reason why recorders, strings and other 'c' instruments should not be included. If a selection of several rounds are performed in a concert, vary the instrumentation.

Any of the INSTRUMENTAL or VOICE parts may be omitted from the OSTINATO. The rounds may also be sung unaccompanied, in which case it will be necessary to play a starting note. A useful performance plan is as follows:

1. PIANO plays 4 bar OSTINATO once (or 2 bars twice) alone.
2. PERCUSSION INSTRUMENTS join in OSTINATO in turn.
3. VOICES join in the OSTINATO and continue into the round.The round is sung once in unison, then three times in parts.

Key

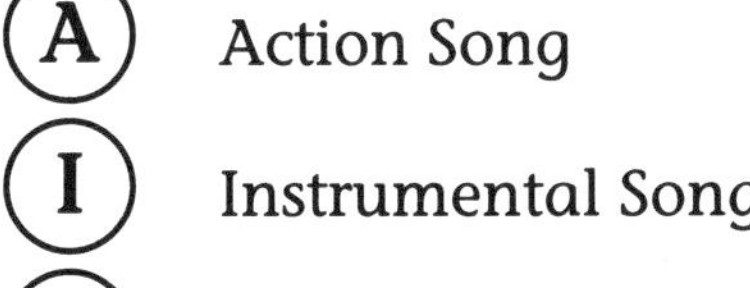

(A) Action Song

(I) Instrumental Song

(R) Round

(P) Part Song

(S) Song just for singing

Material suitable for pre-school.

Material suitable for key stage one.

Material suitable for key stage two.

Arm Movements

Words and Music by
Eileen Diamond

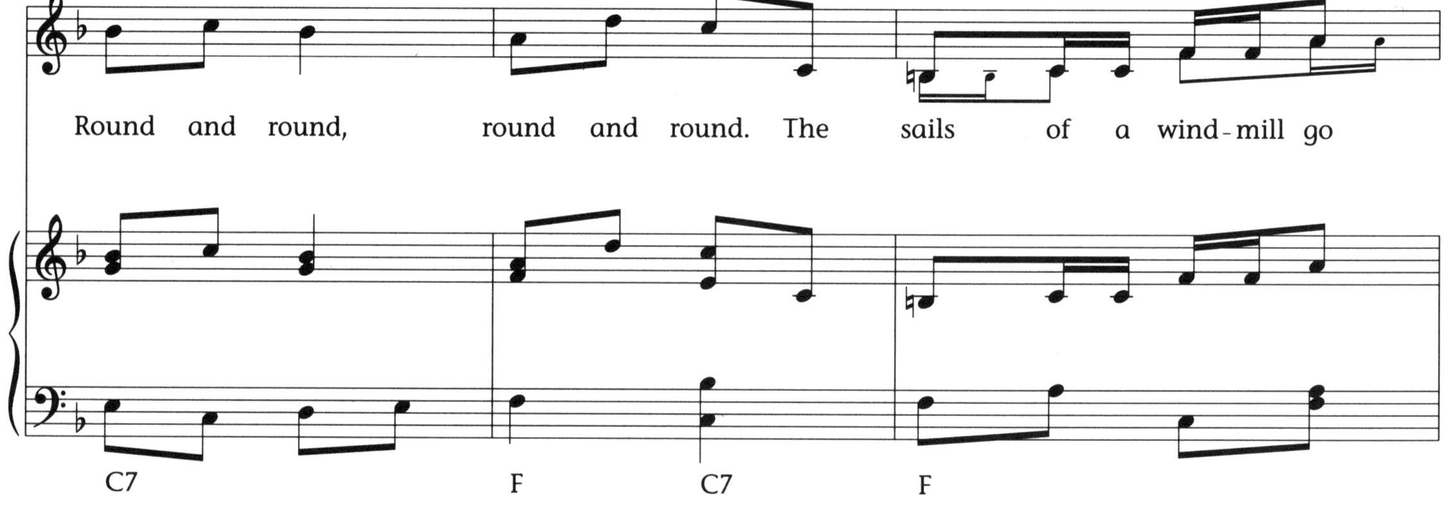

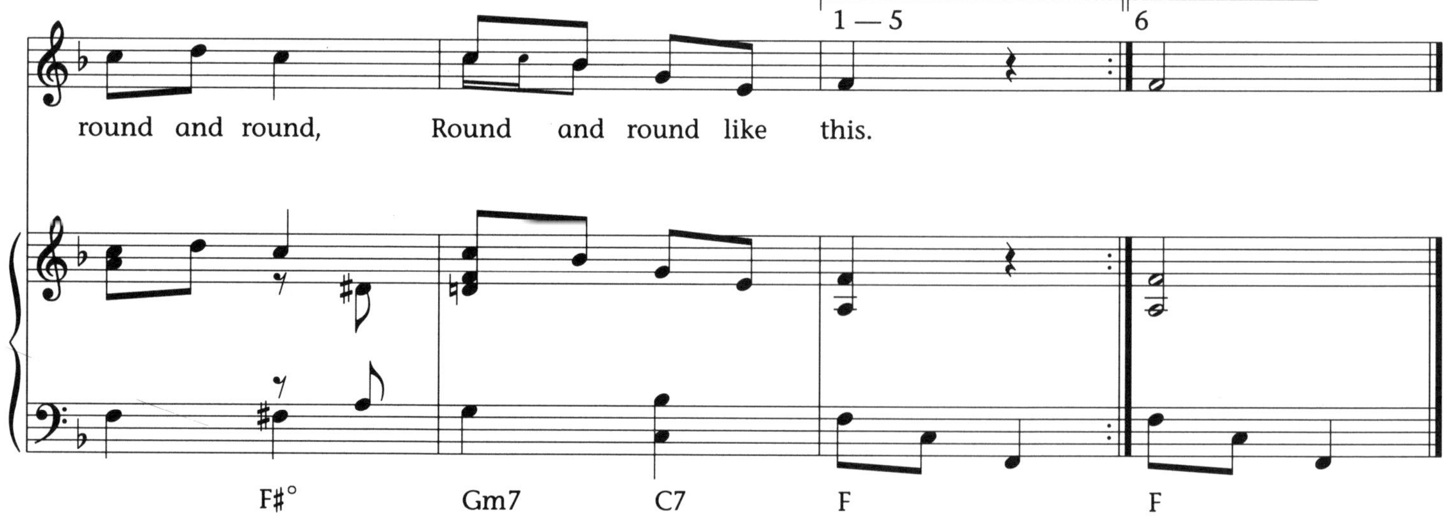

1. The sails of a windmill go round and round,
Round and round, round and round.
The sails of a windmill go round and round,
Round and round like this.

2. A see-saw goes way up and down,
Up and down, up and down.
A see-saw goes way up and down,
Up and down like this.

3. The branches of a tree sway in the breeze,
In the breeze, in the breeze.
The branches of a tree sway in the breeze,
Sway in the breeze like this.

4. A conductor beats the time like this,
Time like this, time like this.
A conductor beats the time like this,
Beats the time like this.

5. A soldier marches with his arms held straight,
Arms held straight, arms held straight.
A soldier marches with his arms held straight,
Arms held straight like this.

6. A butterfly flutters its wings all day,
Wings all day, wings all day.
A butterfly flutters its wings all day,
Flutters its wings like this.

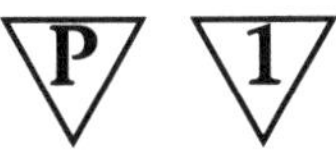

TEACHING IDEAS

An imaginative action song which includes lots of opportunities for rhythmic movement and relates to living experiences.

Performance

Ask the children to stand an arm's length apart and use arm movements only, to illustrate the various verses.

Further discussion and development ideas

Ask the children to suggest other verses using different arm movements.
The following are a few suggestions, the children will no doubt have many more:

A swimmer moves through the water like this . . .

A policeman controls the traffic like this . . .

We exercise our arms like this . . .

Chase Your Cares Away

Words and Music by
Eileen Diamond

Lively

Clap your hands,

F Bb C7 F F

stamp your feet, Hap - py feel - ing, hap - py beat. Clap your hands,

Bb C7 F

Fine

stamp your feet, Chase your cares a - way. If you're feel - ing

Bb B♮° C7 F G7

sad, If you're feel - ing down, Take the feel - ing,

C G7 C A7

Clap your hands, stamp your feet,
Happy feeling, happy beat.
Clap your hands, stamp your feet,
Chase your cares away.

If you're feeling sad,
If you're feeling down,
Take the feeling, wrap it up,
Chase it out of town.

TEACHING IDEAS

A useful action song for introducing rhythm and pulse with opportunities to express emotions to music.

Performance

Combining the strong opening beats with actions will help the children feel the rhythm and pulse of the music. Try the following actions throughout the song:

Clap your hands	clap
Stamp your feet	stamp
Happy feeling, happy beat	sway rhythmically
Clap your hands	clap
Stamp your feet	stamp
Chase your cares away	push hands outwards from centre of body
If you're feeling sad	run fingers down cheeks
If you're feeling down	push hands slowly down
Take the feeling	cup hands and pretend to hold something
Wrap it up	roll hands round and round
Chase it out of town	push hands outwards from centre of body or run on the spot

Further discussion and development ideas

After performing the song straight through, repeat the first eight bars from 𝄋 at a much faster speed.

Dancing In The Garden

Words and Music by
Eileen Diamond

Happily

rit.

C Dm7 G7 C Dm G7 C G7

a tempo

1. One hap - py dan - cer
2. Two hap - py dan - cers

dan - cing in the gar - den, Round and round and round.

C Dm7 G7 C G7

Choose a part - ner and
All join in now and

dance a - round to - ge - ther, Round and round and

(Last Verse:)

C Dm7 Em Dm C Dm G7

round.

rit.

C G7

Last Verse

Now ev - ery - one is dan - cing in the gar - den,

a tempo

C Dm7 G7

Round and round and round. We've all joined hands and we'll dance a-round to-ge - ther,

C G7 C Dm7 G7

Round and round and round and round and round and round and round and round.

C C#° Dm7 D#° C G7 C G7 C

1. One happy dancer dancing in the garden,
Round and round and round.
Choose a partner and dance around together,
Round and round and round.

Last Verse: Eight happy dancers dancing in the garden,
Round and round and round.
All join in now and dance around together,
Round and round and round.

Now everyone is dancing in the garden,
Round and round and round.
We've all joined hands and we'll dance around together,
Round and round and round and round and round and round and round.

TEACHING IDEAS

A useful song for involving the whole class. The mathematical element also makes the song ideal for a cross-curricular link.

Performance

Choose one child to be the first dancer. At *Choose a partner* he or she then chooses a partner, the music pauses to allow time. They then dance around together holding hands. When *Choose a partner* is reached the second time then each child chooses a partner and dances first as a twosome and then at the words *Four happy dancers,* verse 3, they join up in a circle holding hands with the others. The song continues with the number of dancers doubling at each verse. Sing the last verse when a suitable number of children are left, or when the song has gone on long enough. The remaining children join in and dance, everyone holding hands in a large circle. When the song ends the children stand still.

Driving Along On a Big Red Bus

Words and Music by
Eileen Diamond

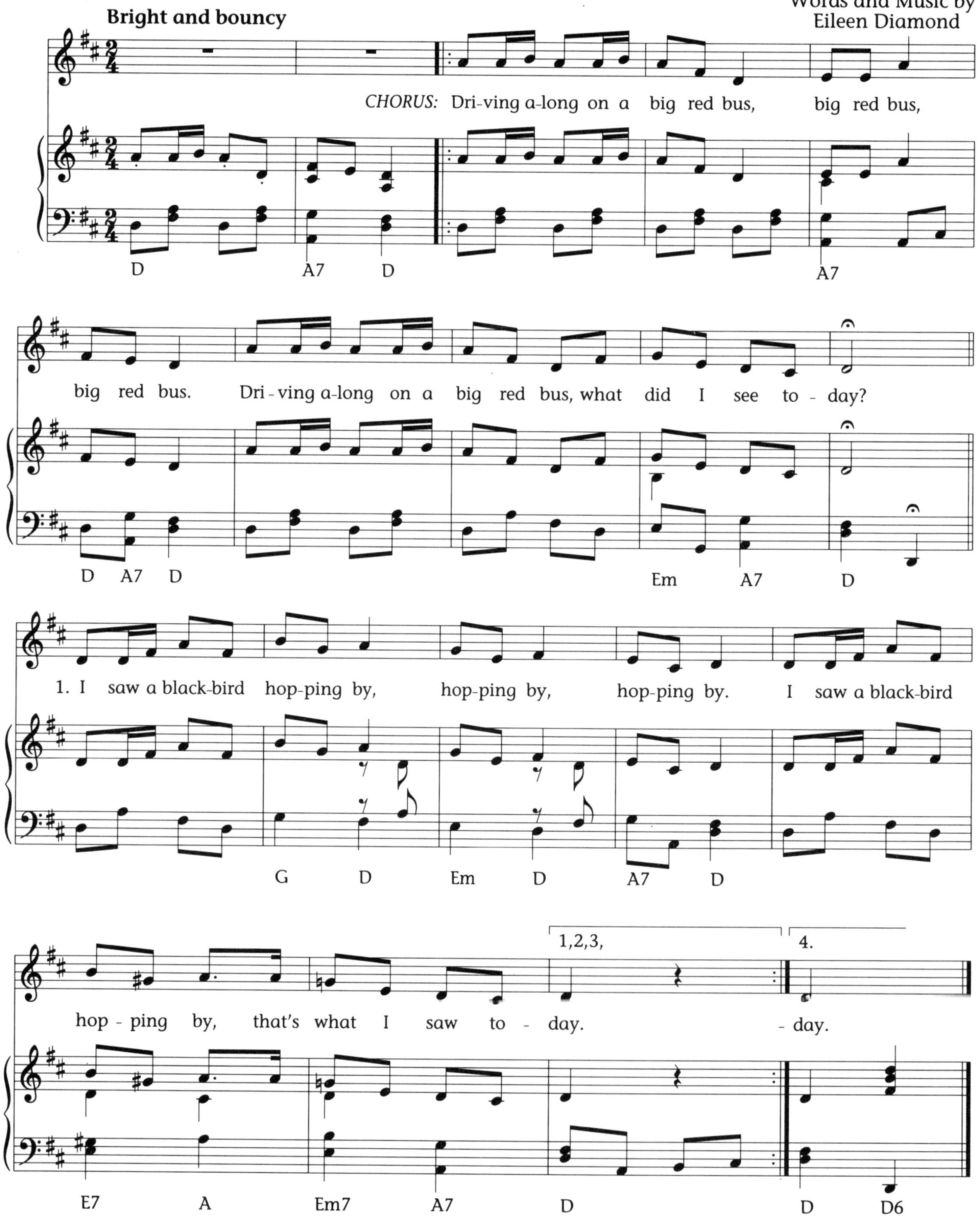

Bright and bouncy

CHORUS: Dri-ving a-long on a big red bus, big red bus,

D A7 D A7

big red bus. Dri - ving a-long on a big red bus, what did I see to - day?

D A7 D Em A7 D

1. I saw a black-bird hop-ping by, hop-ping by, hop-ping by. I saw a black-bird

G D Em D A7 D

1,2,3, 4.

hop - ping by, that's what I saw to - day. - day.

E7 A Em7 A7 D D D6

CHORUS: Driving along on a big red bus, big red bus, big red bus.
Driving along on a big red bus, what did I see today?

1. I saw a blackbird hopping by, hopping by, hopping by.
I saw a blackbird hopping by, that's what I saw today.

CHORUS

2. I saw a plane go flying by, *etc.*

CHORUS

3. I saw some soldiers marching by, *etc.*

CHORUS

4. I saw a train go rattling by, *etc.*

TEACHING IDEAS

A song that relates to children's daily experiences and helps to stimulate their imagination.

Performance

Everyone sings the chorus, then one, or more of the children perform the actions while the rest of the children continue to sing. In verse four get several children to hold on to each other to imitate the train.

Further discussion and development ideas

Ask the children for further answers to *What did I see today? and* fit them to the music. Here are a few suggestions:

Some children playing ball

People digging their gardens

Rabbits hopping by

Some cars go under a bridge

For a concert performance, divide the class into two groups. The first group sit in a row of pairs as though on a bus. The other group perform the actions. After a few verses, the groups change over.

Fingers And Thumbs

Words and Music by
Eileen Diamond

Relaxed and not too fast

There's one thumb on this hand And one thumb on that; They're not quite like fin - gers, They're just a lit - tle bit fat. Now wrig-gle your thumbs, Twid-dle your thumbs, There's one thumb on this hand And one thumb on that. Thumbs and fin - gers, Fin - gers and

Em D A7 D A7 D Bm D/A Em
A7 D Bm E7 Am7 D7
G A7 D D7 B7 Em
G#° D/A F#7 Bm Gm6 D/A A7

thumbs. There are four fin - gers on
D Em D A7 D A7 D
this hand And four fin-gers on that; They're not quite like thumbs, They are
Bm D/A Em A7 D Bm
not quite so fat. Now wrig - gle your fin - gers,
E7 Am7 D7 G A7
Twid-dle your fin - gers, There are four fin - gers on this hand And
D D7 B7 Em G♯°

	Actions
1. There's one thumb on this hand	Hold up one thumb
And one thumb on that;	Hold up other thumb
They're not quite like fingers,	Hold up fingers
They're just a little bit fat.	Hold up thumbs
Now wriggle your thumbs,	Wriggle thumbs
Twiddle your thumbs,	Twiddle thumbs
There's one thumb on this hand	Hold up one thumb
And one thumb on that.	Hold up other thumb
Thumbs and fingers,	Hold up thumbs, then fingers
Fingers and thumbs.	Hold up fingers, then thumbs.

2. There are four fingers on this hand
And four fingers on that;
They're not quite like thumbs,
They are not quite so fat.
Now wriggle your fingers,
Twiddle your fingers,
There are four fingers on this hand
And four fingers on that.
Thumbs and fingers,
Fingers and thumbs.
Fingers and thumbs,
Fingers and thumbs.

TEACHING IDEAS

A simple hand action song for the very young. The song is ideal for creating a quiet interlude between more active songs.

Performance

Make the actions positive and show the children how to hide their thumbs behind palms when holding up four fingers. For *Twiddle your fingers* rotate hands around each other. Keep the tempo relaxed to allow the fingers and thumbs to sort themselves out and give the children time to respond and react. As the actions and words combine, the co-ordination will improve.

Further discussion and development ideas

Talk about the use of the fingers and thumbs:

Fingers - touch/feel
pick up objects
point
beckon
play a musical instrument
fingerprints

Thumbs - help to grip
turn pages of a book
carry things

Ask the children to add to the list. Ask the children about finger and thumb language:

Fingers - on lips (be quiet)
to head (thinking)
in ears (too loud)

Thumbs - upwards (good sign)
downwards (bad sign)

Here's A Rhythm

Words and Music by
Eileen Diamond

Bright and rhythmic

Here's a rhy - thm, you can clap it with your

G G7 C G7 C C#°

hands, *(CLAP)* With your hands, *(CLAP)* with your hands. *(CLAP)* Here's a

Dm Dm7 G7 C G7

rhy - thm, you can clap it with your hands, *(CLAP)* With your hands, *(CLAP)* with your

C C#° Dm D#° Em G7

hands. *(CLAP)* Now, try a dif - ferent rhy - thm.

C C+ F G7 C

(TEACHER CLAPS)
(CHILDREN CLAP OR PLAY)
Here's a - no - ther one to
E7
fol - low.
(TEACHER CLAPS)
(CHILDREN CLAP OR PLAY)
Am
D7
Now let's play a rhy - thm on the tam - bour-ines, (TAMBOURINES) Then the
G7
C
C#°
Dm
Dm7
drums, (DRUMS) then the bells. (BELLS) Now the wood blocks and the claves can play it
G7
C
G7
C
C#°

Here's a rhythm, you can clap it with your hands, (CLAP)
With your hands, (CLAP) with your hands. (CLAP)
Here's a rhythm, you can clap it with your hands, (CLAP)
With your hands, (CLAP) with your hands. (CLAP)

Now, try a different rhythm, (TEACHER CLAPS) (CHILDREN CLAP OR PLAY)
Here's another one to follow. (TEACHER CLAPS) (CHILDREN CLAP OR PLAY)

Now let's play a rhythm on the tambourines, (TAMBOURINES)
Then the drums, (DRUMS) then the bells. (BELLS)
Now the wood blocks and the claves can play it too, (WOODBLOCKS & CLAVES)
And we'll all play together at the end. (ALL)

TEACHING IDEAS

A song to encourage children to listen and then be able to recall a rhythm by playing or clapping it back.

Performance

INSTRUMENTS: TAMBOURINES, DRUMS, BELLS, WOODBLOCKS, CLAVES.
Distribute a number of instruments among half of the class. Ask the other half to clap. Any rhythm may be used after the words *Now try another rhythm* and *Here's another one to follow.* All the children join in repeating the rhythm either by clapping or playing their instruments.

Further discussion and development ideas

When the song is familiar, get the children to improvise by making up their own rhythms for other children to play and clap.

Musical Instruments

Words and Music by
Eileen Diamond

Brightly

F Dm C7 F Dm C7

Band etc.

CHORUS

Mu - si-cal in - stru-ments, mu - si-cal in - stru-ments, It's such fun to

F Gm G7 C7

Last time to Coda

play up-on an in - stru-ment. Mu - si-cal in - stru-ments, mu - si-cal in - stru-ments,

F C7 F B♭ B°

See what there is to play.

C7 F C7 F Dm C7

Solo

1. Play a gui - tar, play a gui - tar,
2. Play a trom - bone, play a trom - bone,

F Dm C7 F D7 Gm

You play like this, chung-a-chung, chung-a-chung, When you play a gui - tar.
You play like this, with a slide and a glide, When you play a trom - bone.

G7 C7 F B°

CODA

They're such fun to play.

C7 C7 F

CHORUS Musical instruments, musical instruments,
It's such fun to play upon an instrument.
Musical instruments, musical instruments,
See what there is to play.

1. Play a guitar, play a guitar,
You play like this, chung-a-chung, chung-a-chung,
When you play a guitar.

CHORUS

2. Play a trombone, play a trombone,
You play like this, with a slide and a glide,
When you play a trombone.

CHORUS

3. Play a violin, play a violin,
You play like this, move a bow to and fro *etc.*

CHORUS

4. Play on a flute, play on a flute,
You play like this, toot-a-toot, toot-a-toot *etc.*

CHORUS

Ask the children to make up other verses using different instruments.

TEACHING IDEAS

A topical song covering a wide range of musical instruments and offering several performance possibilities.

Performance

Mime the actions needed to play the various instruments in each of the verses.

Alternatively, substitute the tuned instruments in the verses for percussion ones. Divide into groups for the verses and all play together for the chorus.

For example:

Play on the drums
Play on the bells
Play the tambourines

Another idea is to ask the children to take it in turns to think of a musical instrument and pretend to play it in front of the others while they sing the following:

Guess what he's/she's playing, guess what he's/she's playing
He/she plays like this.
Can we guess what he's/she's playing?

The music then pauses. Make sure there's no calling out! The children put up their hands if they think they can name the instrument and the player chooses someone to say what it was. Whoever gets it right has a turn at being the player. The chorus may be accompanied by playing or clapping.

Further discussion and development ideas

Try to find some pictures of orchestral instruments and talk about the different families such as strings, woodwind, brass, percussion. Discuss the different ways in which they are played and the sounds they produce.

Listen To Me

Words and Music by
Eileen Diamond

Gently, with a lilt

A lit - tle green frog leapt o - ver a hill And lan - ded on a win - dow sill. 'Croak croak', said he, 'Croak croak', said he, 'Lis - ten to me'.

G7 C E7 F A7 Dm G C A7 Dm G7 C

Last verse to 𝄌 *Coda*

𝄌 **CODA**

G7 C

1. A little green frog leapt over a hill
   And landed on a window sill.
   'Croak croak,' said he, 'Croak croak,' said he,
   'Listen to me.'

2. A little black bird flew over the hill
   And landed on a window sill.
   'Chirp chirp,' said he, 'Chirp chirp,' said he,
   'Listen to me.'

3. A little white cat ran over the hill
   And landed on a window sill.
   'Miaow,' said he, 'Miaow,' said he,
   'Listen to me.'

4. A little grey mouse crept over the hill
   And landed on a window sill.
   'Squeak squeak,' said he, 'Squeak squeak,' said he,
   'Listen to me.'

5. A little bright boy leapt out of his bed
   And from the window popped his head.
   'Good morning,' said he, 'Good morning,' said he,
   'Listen to me.'

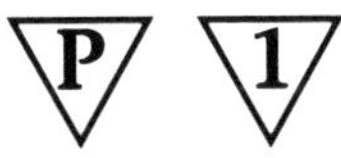

TEACHING IDEAS

A gentle and tuneful song suitable for early learning.

Performance

The last two lines of each verse could be repeated to allow the children to join in with animal sounds. In verse five, the word *boy* may be changed to *girl* if wished and the pronouns changed accordingly.

After singing the song for the first time, see if the children can remember the order in which the animals come. Get them to clap the repeated rhythmic pattern of the opening phrase:

Further discussion and development ideas

Use the song to tie in with nature projects. Ask the children what other creatures they might see coming over the hill and the sounds they would make. Perhaps their ideas could fit into another verse.

I

Play A Rhythm

Words and Music by
Eileen Diamond

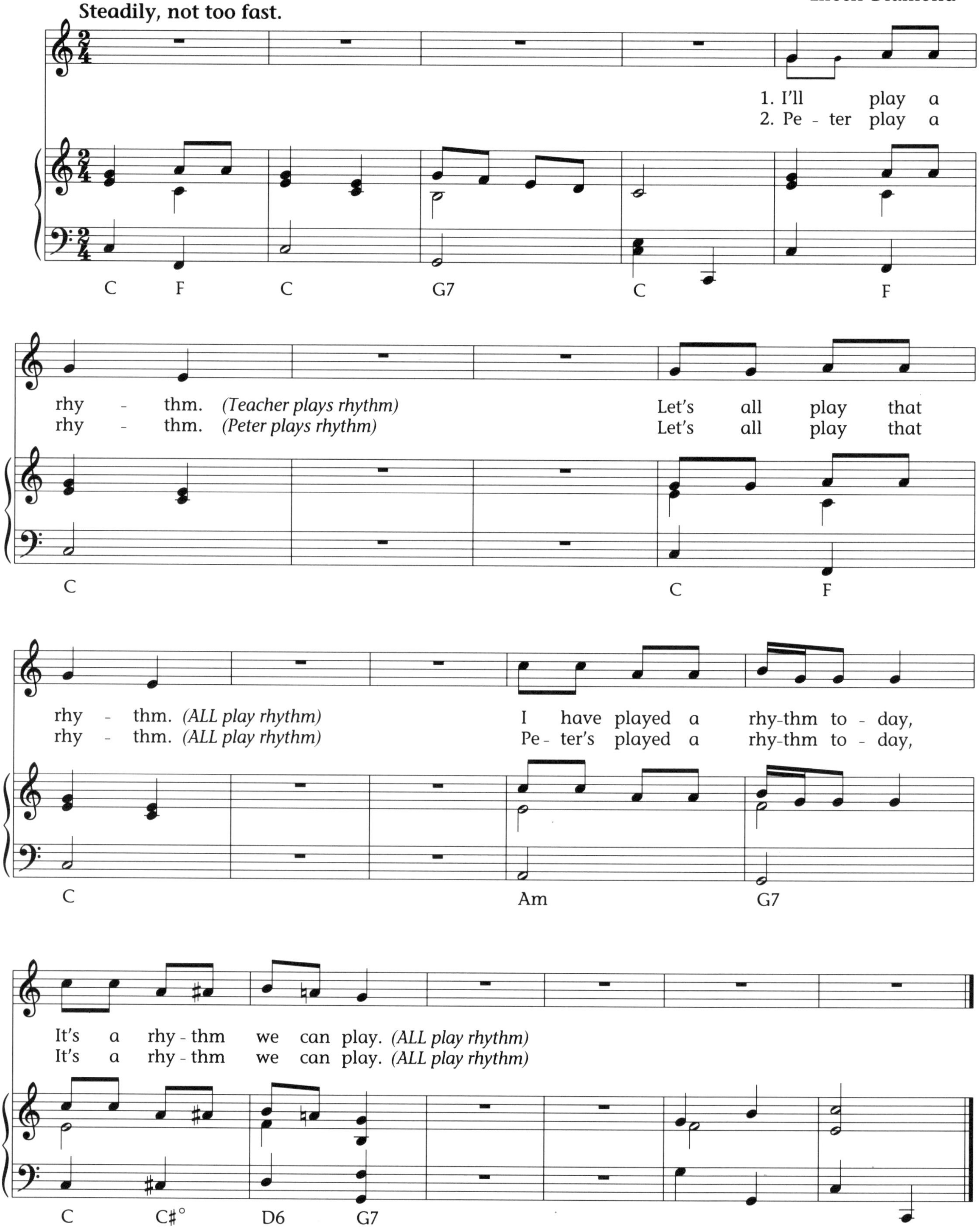

Steadily, not too fast.

1. I'll play a
2. Pe - ter play a

C F C G7 C F

rhy - thm. *(Teacher plays rhythm)* Let's all play that
rhy - thm. *(Peter plays rhythm)* Let's all play that

C C F

rhy - thm. *(ALL play rhythm)* I have played a rhy-thm to - day,
rhy - thm. *(ALL play rhythm)* Pe - ter's played a rhy-thm to - day,

C Am G7

1. I'll play a rhythm. (Teacher plays rhythm)
   Let's all play that rhythm. (ALL play rhythm)
   I have played a rhythm today,
   It's a rhythm we can play. (ALL play rhythm)

2. Peter play a rhythm. (Peter plays rhythm)
   Let's all play that rhythm. (ALL play rhythm)
   Peter's played a rhythm today,
   It's a rhythm we can play. (ALL play rhythm)

TEACHING IDEAS

A song which offers opportunities for children to memorise and imitate short rhythmic patterns by clapping or playing percussion instruments and then to go on and improvise some themselves.

Performance

Although a piano accompaniment is provided, this song is equally effective if it is sung unaccompanied. Choose a variety of percussion instruments and distribute them among the children. The teacher should begin the song by either clapping or playing a made up rhythm. The children then respond with *Let's all play that rhythm* and copy that rhythm on their instruments (or clapping). The song may be repeated as many times as wished with the children taking turns to make up a rhythm.

Here are some rhythmic suggestions:

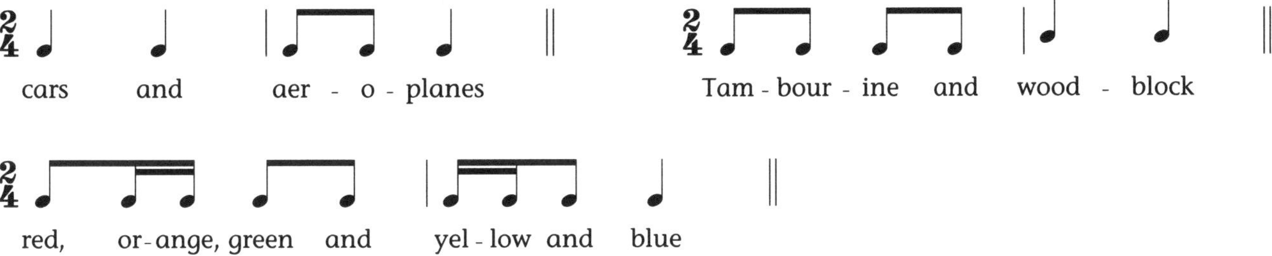

Further discussion and development ideas

Putting words to rhythms makes them easier for children to absorb. Ask the children to think of words to fit the rhythms that they have improvised.

INSTRUMENTS: A VARIETY OF PERCUSSION INSTRUMENTS.

The Snowman

Words and Music by
Eileen Diamond

Cheerfully

F C7 F Bb D7 Gm C7 F

Let's make a snow - man and let's make him fat. Give him a round head and

F C7 F Bb G7 C7 F C7 F

put on a hat. A car - rot for his nose and then I sup-pose, Some

poco rit. *a tempo*

G7sus C7 Am7 D+ D7 Gm7 C7

but - tons down his chest, Oh he real - ly is the best! For he's a fat jol - ly snow - man, A

F D+ D7 Gm G7 C7 F C7 F

Let's make a snowman and let's make him fat.
Give him a round head and put on a hat.
A carrot for his nose and then I suppose,
Some buttons down his chest, Oh he really is the best!
For he's a fat jolly snowman,
A roly poly snowman,
We've made a snowman today.

TEACHING IDEAS

A fun song for young children with descriptive actions to express to the music.

Performance

Add the following actions to the words of the music:

Let's make a snowman	the children begin to dig snow
Let's make him fat	hold arms in a circle in front of body
Give him a round head	draw a circle in the air
Put on a hat	pretend to put on a hat
A carrot for his nose	hold stretched out finger in front of nose
Some buttons down his chest	point to buttons down chest
Oh, he really is the best	hands on hips
Fat jolly snowman	hold arms in a circle in front of body
A roly-poly snowman	roll hands around each other
We've made a snowman today	clap hands

Further discussion and development ideas

Use this song to tie with seasonal topics such as the weather, winter, snow, etc. Ask the children to paint a picture of the snowman in the song.

The Toothbrush Song

Words and Music by
Eileen Diamond

Slow

Ev - ery - bod - y has a tooth - brush,

D7 G C#° G

Ev - ery - bod - y us - es one, But some - times you feel a lit - tle

D7 B7

la - zy, And there's not e - nough brush - ing done. Brush your

Em Em7 A A7 Am7 D7sus D7

Lively
teeth af - ter break - fast, Brush your teeth af - ter lunch, Brush your
G Am A7
teeth ev - ery time that you munch and you crunch. Af - ter tea af - ter sup-per, Move that
D G D7 G
tooth - brush a - bout, It's the best way of mak-ing sure your teeth won't fall out! So
Am B7 Em Am D7 G D7
scrub-a - dub - a - dub - a - dub - a - dub, Let's make our teeth real - ly shine,
G D7

Scrub-a-dub-a-dub-a-dub-a-dub, You do yours and I'll do mine.
G
Up and down and all a-round the sides, To reach the back you o-pen wide, And
B7
Em
scrub-a-dub-a-dub-a-dub-a-dub, Scrub-a-dub-a-dub-dub, dub, dub, Oh,,
Am
D7
G
F#°
F♮°
E7
scrub-a-dub-a-dub-a-dub-a-dub, Scrub-a-dub-a-dub-dub!
Am
D7
G
D7
8va
G

Everybody has a toothbrush,
Everybody uses one,
But sometimes you feel a little lazy,
And there's not enough brushing done,

Brush you teeth after breakfast,
Brush your teeth after lunch,
Brush your teeth every time that you munch and you crunch.
After tea after supper, move that toothbrush about,
It's the best way of making sure you're teeth won't fall out!

So scrub-a-dub-a-dub-a-dub-a-dub,
Let's make our teeth really shine,
Scrub-a-dub-a-dub-a-dub-a-dub,
You do yours and I'll do mine.

Up and down and all around the sides,
To reach the back you open wide,
And scrub-a-dub-a-dub-a-dub-a-dub,
Scrub-a-dub-a-dub-dub,dub,dub,
Oh, scrub-a-dub-a-dub-a-dub-a-dub,
Scrub-a-dub-a-dub-dub!

TEACHING IDEAS

A fun to sing song with rhythmic actions.

Performance

Ask the children to do a rhythmic brushing action with one hand while singing *Scrub-a-dub-a-dub-a-dub-a-dub.*

Further discussion and development ideas

A useful song for topic work and introducing the importance of health and hygiene.

Listen To The Band

Words and Music by
Eileen Diamond

Steadily

D7 B7 Em D A7

DRUMS *etc.*

D D D♯° B7 Em A

1. Lis - ten to the bea - ting of the big bass drums,

A7 D A7 D D7

Lis - ten to the bea - ting of the big bass drums. Lis - ten to the bea - ting of the

B7 Em Gm6 D A7 D

big bass drums.

1 — 3 | 4

1. Listen to the beating of the big bass drums. . .
2. Listen to the rattle of the tambourines. . .
3. Listen to the tinkling of the triangles. . .
4. Listen to the band it's playing quietly now,
   Listen to the band it's playing quietly now,
   Listen to the band it's playing louder now.

TEACHING IDEAS

A useful song for learning about contrasting dynamics, controlling percussion instruments and timbre.

Performance

After the introduction each instrument plays crotchet (quarter note) beats in turn to the appropriate verse. There should be a slight stress on the first beat of each bar, with the second beat played a little lighter, within a steady pulse. Demonstrate this to the children and get them to practice it a few times.

Practice playing quietly, then louder for the end of the song. Explain to the children that playing louder does not mean attacking the instruments with such force that they damage them! Ask them to listen carefully and control their playing so as to obtain a clear contrast between loud and quiet.

Further discussion and development ideas

Other instruments may also be used and extra verses added to discuss the sound each instrument makes.

For example:

Listen to the swishing of the shakers now.
Listen to the jingling of the jingle bells.

Ask the children to make up another verse using their own ideas.

INSTRUMENTS: DRUMS, TAMBOURINES, TRIANGLES.

The Gardener

Words and Music by
Eileen Diamond

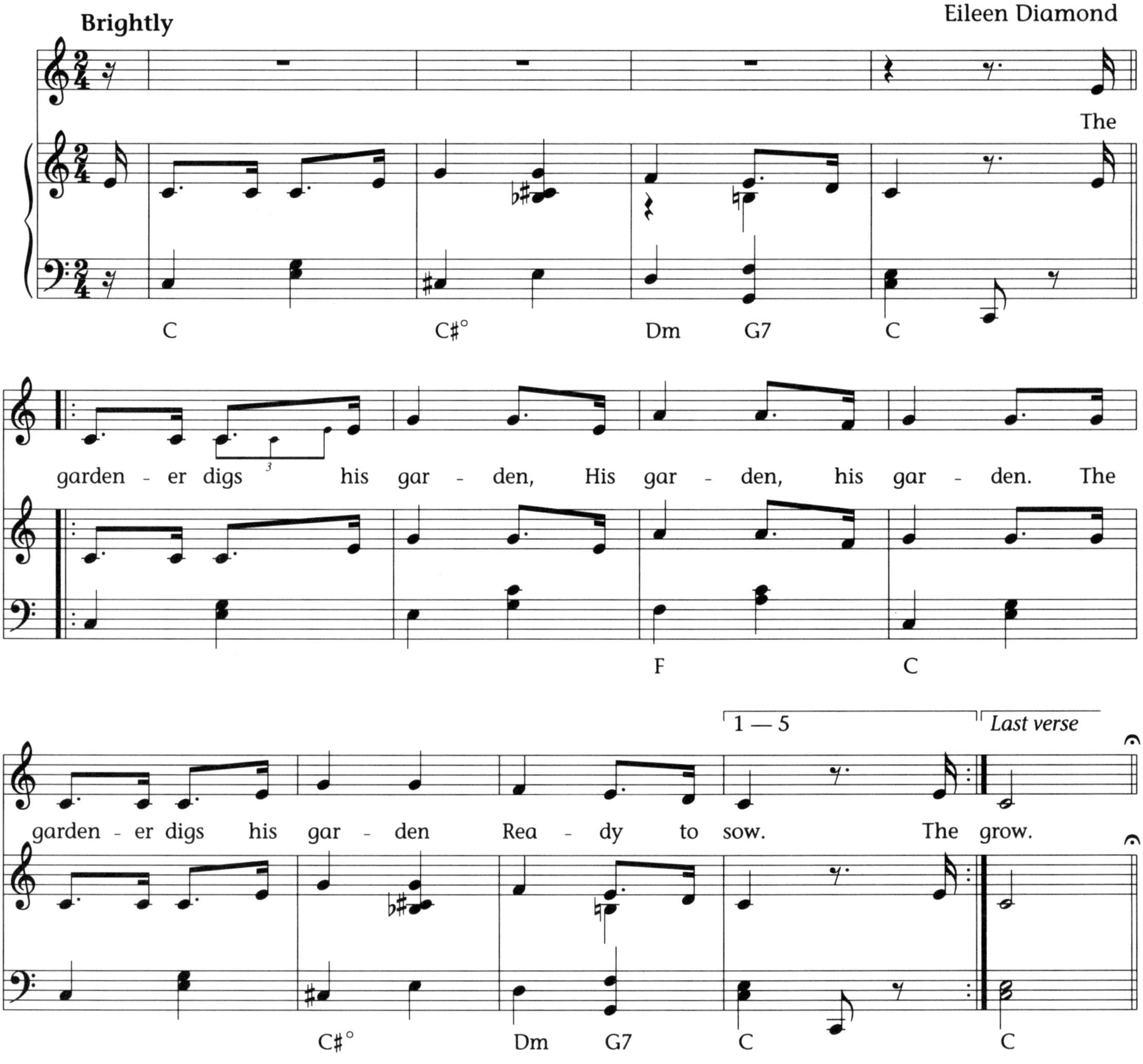

Brightly

The

C C#° Dm G7 C

garden - er digs his gar - den, His gar - den, his gar - den. The

F C

1 — 5 | Last verse

garden - er digs his gar - den Rea - dy to sow. The grow.

C#° Dm G7 C C

Growing Music

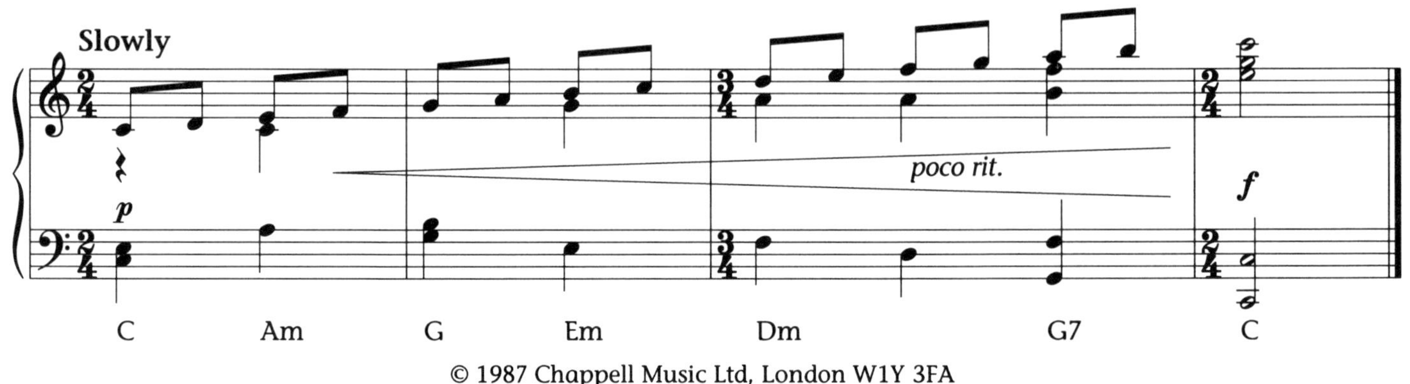

1. The gardener digs his garden,
   His garden, his garden.
   The gardener digs his garden
   Ready to sow.

2. The gardener plants his turnips,
   His turnips, his turnips.
   The gardener plants his turnips
   All in a row.

3. The gardener plants his onions, (*etc*).

4. The gardener plants his carrots, (*etc*).

5. The gardener plants his parsnips, (*etc*).

6. The gardener waters his garden,
   His garden, his garden.
   The gardener waters his garden,
   Now watch it grow!

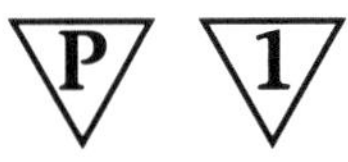

TEACHING IDEAS

A useful performance song with lots of opportunities for cross-curricular links including nature, the environment, food, growth and climate.

Performance

Choose a *Gardener* and decide what sort of garden he/she would like to plant, e.g. vegetables, flowers, fruit, trees, herbs, etc.

Ask the children to name some of the plants in the category chosen.

Select an appropriate number of children to represent each chosen plant and stand them in a line or in groups.

The remainder of the children should sing the song while the *gardener* performs the appropriate *digging, planting* and *watering* actions.

For the planting action the gardener touches each child on both shoulders and the child then crouches down and remains in that position until ready to grow. It's fun to use a real watering can (empty!) if available. After a short pause the *growing music* is played and the plants SLOWLY start to grow, the children stretching as high as they can.

It may help to play the *growing music* to the children before starting the song. Encourage them to listen to how the music rises in pitch. Ask them to time their growing so that they reach their peak at the same time as the music.

Further discussion and development ideas

Talk about root vegetables that grow under the ground and those which grow above the ground. Look at flowers that grow at different times of the year, e.g. daffodils in spring, roses in summer. Discuss the different ways in which plants grow from bulbs, seeds, cuttings, etc.

Clap Your Hands Like This

Words and Music by
Eileen Diamond

Moderately

When the mu - sic be - gins and you feel your-self sway - ing, Here are some things you can do while it's play - ing.

F Am/c Dm Am B♭ F Gm C7

F Am Dm C7 F Dm7

Fairly lively

ritard. *a tempo*

1. Clap your hands like this, Clap your hands like this. Hear the mu - sic play, Let your
2. Snap your fin - gers like this, Snap your fin - gers like this. Hear the mu - sic play, Let your

Gm7 C7 F C7 F

Dm7 G7 C7 F F7

bo - dy sway, While you clap your hands like this. Are you
bo - dy sway, While you snap your fin - gers like this. Are you
Bb Bbm F C7 F F7
clap - ping? Are you clap - ping your hands? Just keep on
snap - ping? Are you snap - ping your fin - gers? Keep on
Bb C7 F F° F Dm7
clap - ping while the mu - sic plays. Are you
snap - ping while the mu - sic plays. Are you
Gm C7 F F7
clap - ping? Are you clap - ping your hands? Just keep on
snap - ping? Are you snap - ping your fin - gers? Keep on
Bb C7 F F° F Dm7

Last time to Coda
A little slower
clap - ping while the mu - sic plays.
snap - ping while the mu - sic plays.
Now some-thing
poco rit.
Gm
C7
F
E7
Moderately
else to do, Try a dif - ferent move-ment.
(*prepare for next action)
A7
Dm
Gm7
C7
F
Am/C
CODA
Just keep on
Dm
Am
B♭
F
Gm
C7
F
Dm7
dan - cing while the mu - sic plays.
Gm7
C7
F
C7
F

When the music begins and you feel yourself swaying,
Here are some things you can do while it's playing.

1. Clap your hands like this,
Clap your hands like this,
Hear the music play,
Let your body sway,
While you clap your hands like this.
Are you clapping?
Are you clapping your hands?
Just keep on clapping while the music plays.
Are you clapping?
Are you clapping your hands?
Just keep on clapping while the music plays.

(All except verse 4) Now something else to do,
Try a different movement.

2. Snap your fingers etc.

3. Swing your arms etc.

4. Dance around etc.
Just keep on dancing while the music plays.

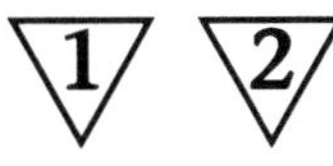

TEACHING IDEAS

A song to encourage different ways of moving to a lively, rhythmic tune.

Performance

Add actions and movements to the words of the song:

Clap your hands
Snap your fingers
Swing your arms
Dance around

Ask the children for more suggestions. After the words *Try a different rhythm* the four bars of piano music may be used to prepare the children for the action in the next verse.

For example:

In the next verse try snapping your fingers
or
What action could we do in the next verse?

If necessary, pause on the last chord to accommodate the children's response and give time to decide on an action.

Little Grey Donkey

Words and Music by
Eileen Diamond

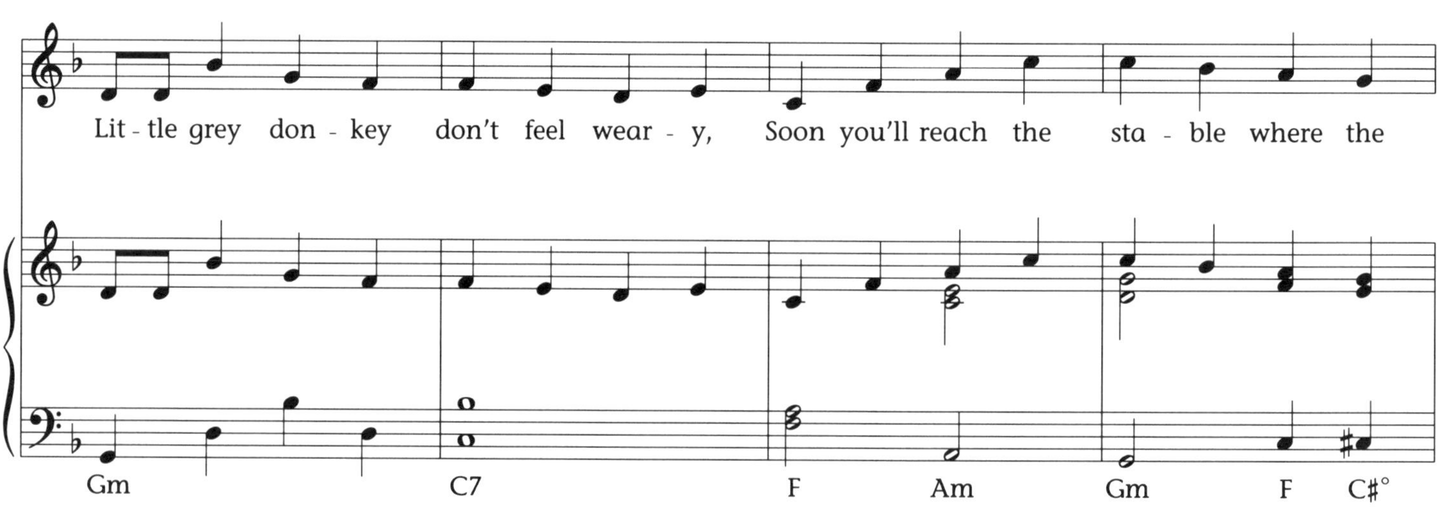

Lit - tle grey don - key bur - den ho - ly, You will be in Beth - le - hem on
Gm C7 F F♯° Gm D7 Gm
Joyful
Christ - mas morn. Shep - herds and kings will come with
mf
C7 F B♭ E♭
gifts from a - far, Led to this ho - ly place by a
F7 B♭ D7 Gm D Gm
bright, shin - ing star. Bells will ring out— re - joice! And
F C7 F G♯° F7 B♭ E♭

trum - pets will sound. An - gel - ic choirs will sing of glo - ry
F7
B♭
A7
Dm
f
Steadily
all a - round. Lit - tle grey don - key you've done your best now,
poco rit.
Quietly a tempo
C G7 C C7 F D7
Lit - tle grey don - key it's time to rest now, Here in - side the sta - ble 'til the
Gm C7 F F7 B♭
light of dawn. Rest be - side the ba - by who will
F C♯° Dm G7 F C° B♭ B♭m

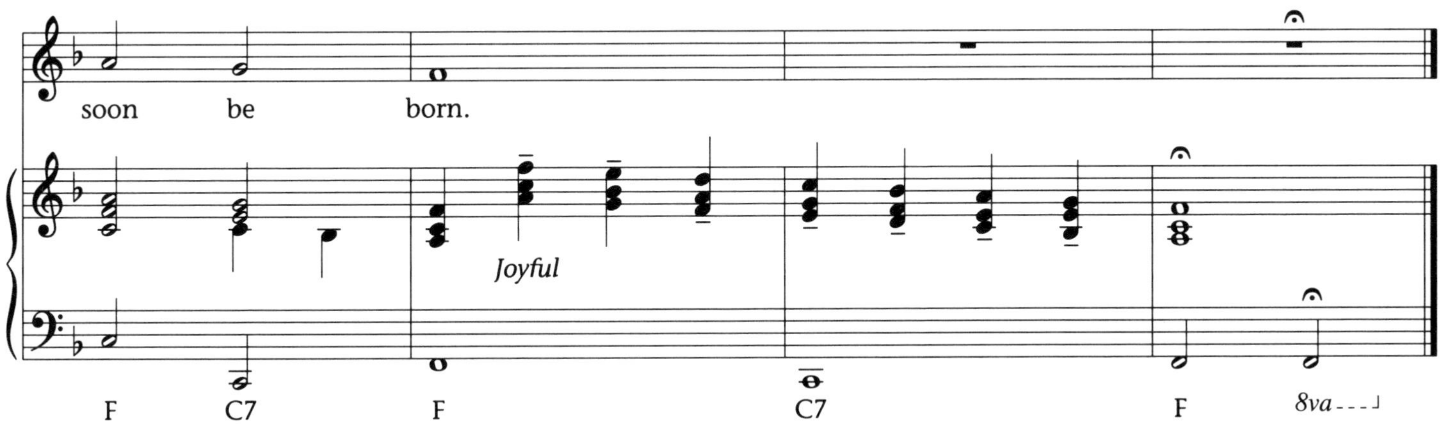

Little grey donkey carrying Mary,
Little grey donkey don't feel weary,
Soon you'll reach the stable
Where the baby will be born.

Little grey donkey travelling slowly,
Little grey donkey burden holy,
You will be in Bethlehem
On Christmas morn.

Shepherds and kings will come with gifts from afar,
Led to this holy place by a bright, shining star,
Bells will ring out – rejoice! And trumpets will sound.
Angelic choirs will sing of glory all around.

Little grey donkey you've done your best now,
Little grey donkey it's time to rest now,
Here inside the stable 'til the light of dawn.
Rest beside the baby who will soon be born.

TEACHING IDEAS

A simple song which tells the Christmas story.

Performance

Make the joyful middle section of the song contrast with the gentle, quiet first and final sections.

Marching Along As We Play

Words and Music by
Eileen Diamond

Steady marching time

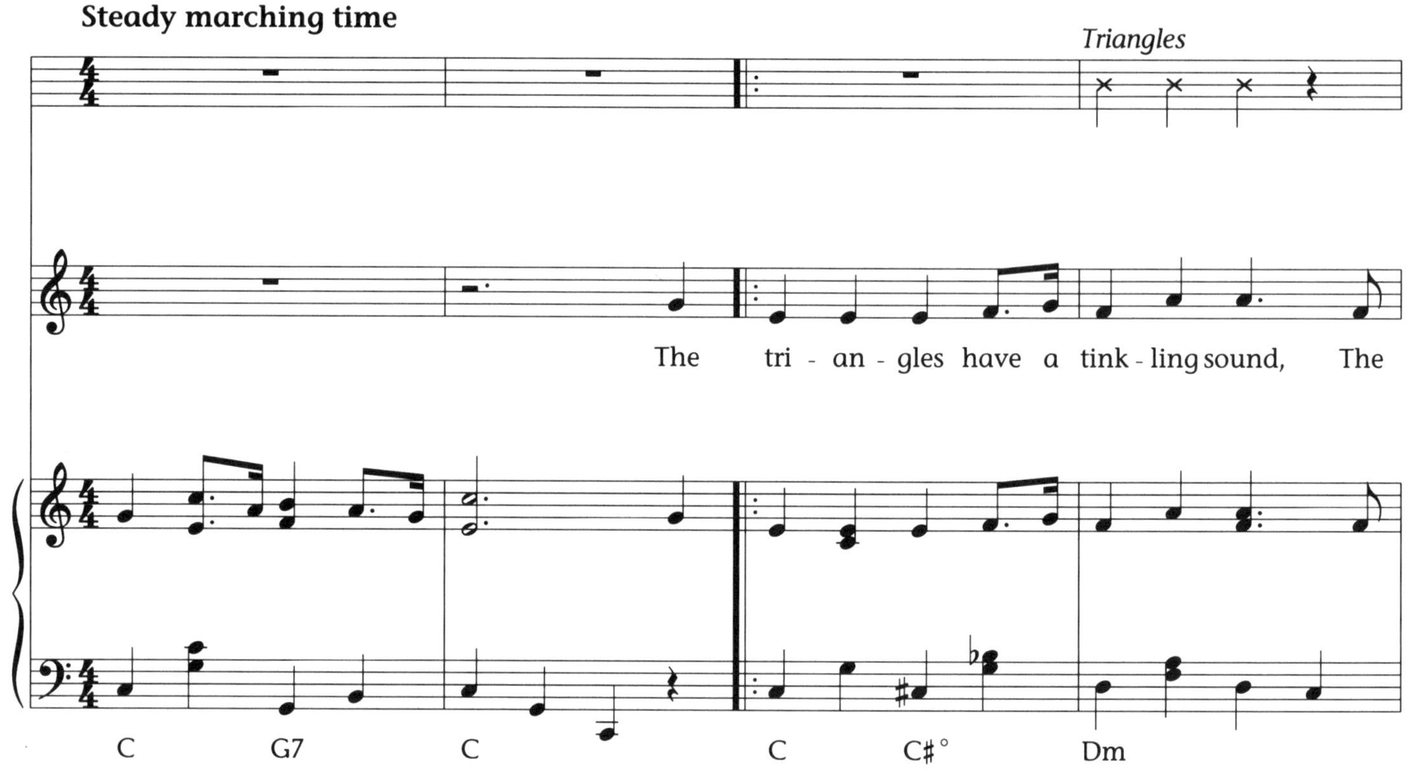

Cymbals
Lis - ten now hear the cym - bals come, Clash! Clash! What a love - ly sound,
D D7 G F#° G7 C Dm
Chime Bars
Clash! Clash! Hear the rhy - thm poun - ding. Ding dong ding hear the chime bars play,
G7 D#° C G7 C C#° Dm
Shakers
All
Ch. Bars
Now all the sha - kers shake a - way. Come on now let ev - ery-bo - dy play to-ge - ther
G Dm7 G7 G7 C G7 C E7 F

The triangles have a tinkling sound,
The tambourines rattle all around.
The drums go rum tiddly um-tum-tum,
Listen now hear the cymbals come,

Clash! Clash! What a lovely sound,
Clash! Clash! Hear the rhythm pounding.
Ding dong ding hear the chime bars play,
Now all the shakers shake away.

Come on now let everybody play together
Marching along as we play.

TEACHING IDEAS

An action song with percussion instruments. The marching style and the instrumental opportunities provide an enjoyable way of combining the skills of rhythm and co-ordination.

Performance

INSTRUMENTS: TRIANGLES, TAMBOURINES, DRUMS, CYMBALS, CHIME BARS (E AND F), SHAKERS. Any number of each instrument may be used.

First the children sing the song and play their instruments at the appropriate moment. On the repeat they march to the music, still playing their instruments at the correct moment, but without singing. This requires great concentration and the children need to listen carefully so that they know where to come in.

Further discussion and development ideas

Ask the children if they have ever watched a marching band, perhaps at local events, or if they have seen any televised state occasions where military bands march and play. Talk about the musical instruments you would find in a marching band.

The Music Band

Words and Music by
Eileen Diamond

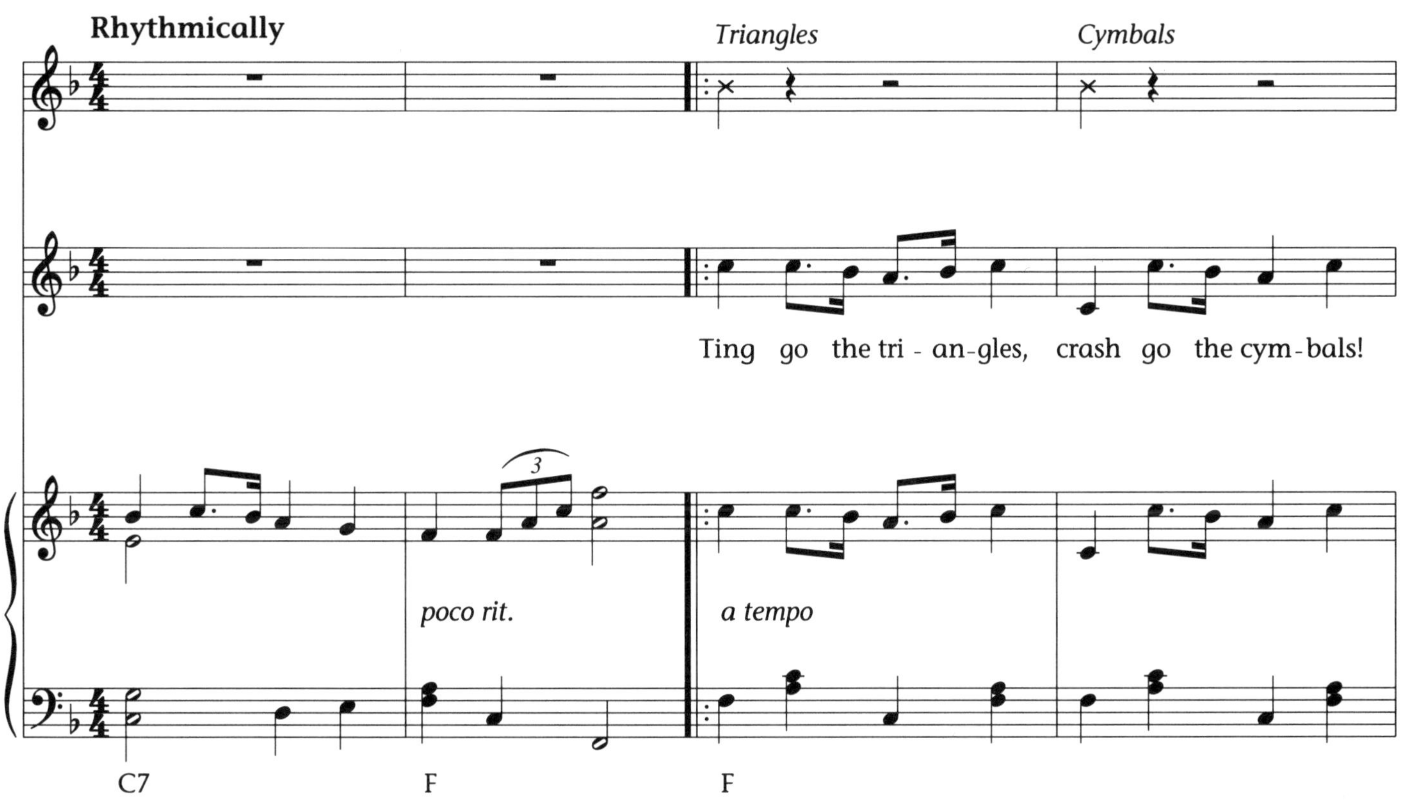

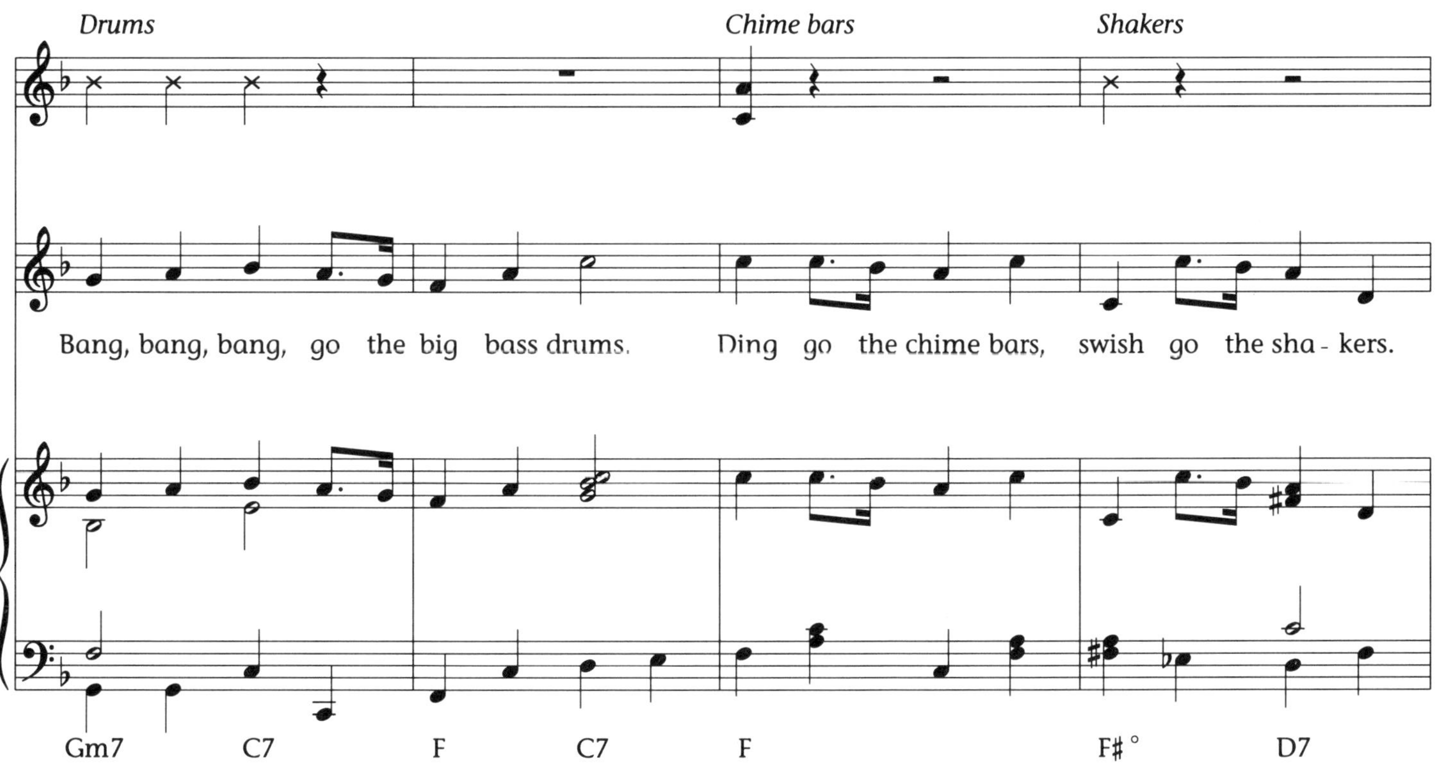

Tambourines
Tap, tap, tap, go the tam - bour - ines. Lis - ten to the mu - sic, lis - ten to the sound,
Gm F♯° Gm C7 F Gm C7 F F♯°
Band
Chime bars
Can you feel the rhy - thm bea - ting all a-round? Oh let's play to-ge - ther now,
Gm C7 F F♯° Gm C7
1
2
Ev - ery-one to-ge - ther now, Join in the mu - sic band. band.
poco rit.
F E♭° D7 Gm C7 F B° C7 C+ F

Ting go the triangles, crash go the cymbals!
Bang, bang, bang, go the big bass drums.
Ding go the chime bars, swish go the shakers.
Tap, tap, tap, go the tambourines.

Listen to the music, listen to the sound,
Can you feel the rhythm beating all around?
Oh let's play together now,
Everyone together now,
Join in the music band.

TEACHING IDEAS

A song for listening, appraising, dynamic control and playing in time.

Performance

INSTRUMENTS: TRIANGLES, CYMBALS, DRUMS, CHIME BARS (C, A AND G), TAMBOURINES, SHAKERS. Any number of instruments may be used.

Get the children to listen carefully and feel the beat so that they play at precisely the right moment. When the song is repeated leave out the words *Ting, crash, bang, ding, swish and tap,* so that the instruments are heard on their own.

Suggest that when they all play together at the end, it may sound nicer if they play their instruments quieter than when they are playing them individually. Experiment with different levels of volume.

Play Your Sound

Words and Music by
Eileen Diamond

Joyfully, with a lilt

Gm C7 F F

1. Tam-bour-ines, tam-bour-ines,
2. Tri - an - gles, tri - an - gles,

a tempo

play your sound. *1. Tambourines*
play your sound. *2. Triangles*

C7 Gm C7 F

Now let's hear ev - ery - one play to - ge - ther.

F7 B♭ B♭m F D7

1,2,3,4

All percussion

Gm C7 F Am

1. Tambourines, tambourines, play your sound.
   (Tambourines)
   Now let's hear everyone play together.
   (All percussion)

2. Triangles etc.

3. Sleigh bells and shakers etc.

4. Scrapers and wood blocks etc.

5. Drums etc.

TEACHING IDEAS

A song which explores the different sounds and timbre of various instruments, played in family groups and mixed together.

INSTRUMENTS: TAMBOURINES, TRIANGLES, BELLS, SHAKERS, SCRAPERS, WOOD BLOCKS, DRUMS.
Any number of each instrument may be used.

Let this song swing along with a slight stress on the first beat of each bar.
Arrange the players in groups according to instruments:

Verse one - tambourines
Verse two - triangles
Verse three - sleigh bells and shakers
Verse four - scrapers and wood blocks
Verse five - drums

Further discussion and development ideas

Discuss the sound different instruments make and the difference in timbre when they play individually, then together.

Playing Quietly

Words and Music by
Eileen Diamond

At a moderate pace

Metallophones
Glockenspiels
Xylophones

Mixed
percussion

p

Play-ing quiet-ly, play-ing quiet-ly, A

Dm A7 Dm A7 Dm A7 Dm A7

lit-tle bit of sound, not more. Now play lou-der, a

poco rit.

mf a tempo

Dm A7 Dm C7 F C7

lit-tle bit lou-der, Let the sound gen-tly soar.

poco rit.

F C7 F Gm7 C F A7

Playing quietly, playing quietly,
A little bit of sound, not more.
Now play louder, a little bit louder,
Let the sound gently soar.
Then get ready to play very loud,
Let's have a mighty roar!

TEACHING IDEAS

A useful song for controlling dynamics.

Performance

Use a reasonable number of mixed percussion instruments. The melodic pattern for the metallophones, glocks and xylophones is:

D A | D A | D A | D – | F C | F C | F C | F – | – | – | C C | F – |

Before learning the song, practise the following exercise:

4/4 ♩ ♩ ♩ ♩ | ♩ ♩ ♩ ♩ ||

1. *p* - quietly
2. *mf* - fairly loud
3. *f* - loud
4. *ff* - very loud

Then try playing with a gradual crescendo:

p *mf* *f* *ff*

Then with a diminuendo:

ff *f* *mf* *p*

Lazin' In The Summer Sun (2 part round)

Words and Music by
Eileen Diamond

Accompaniment Ostinato

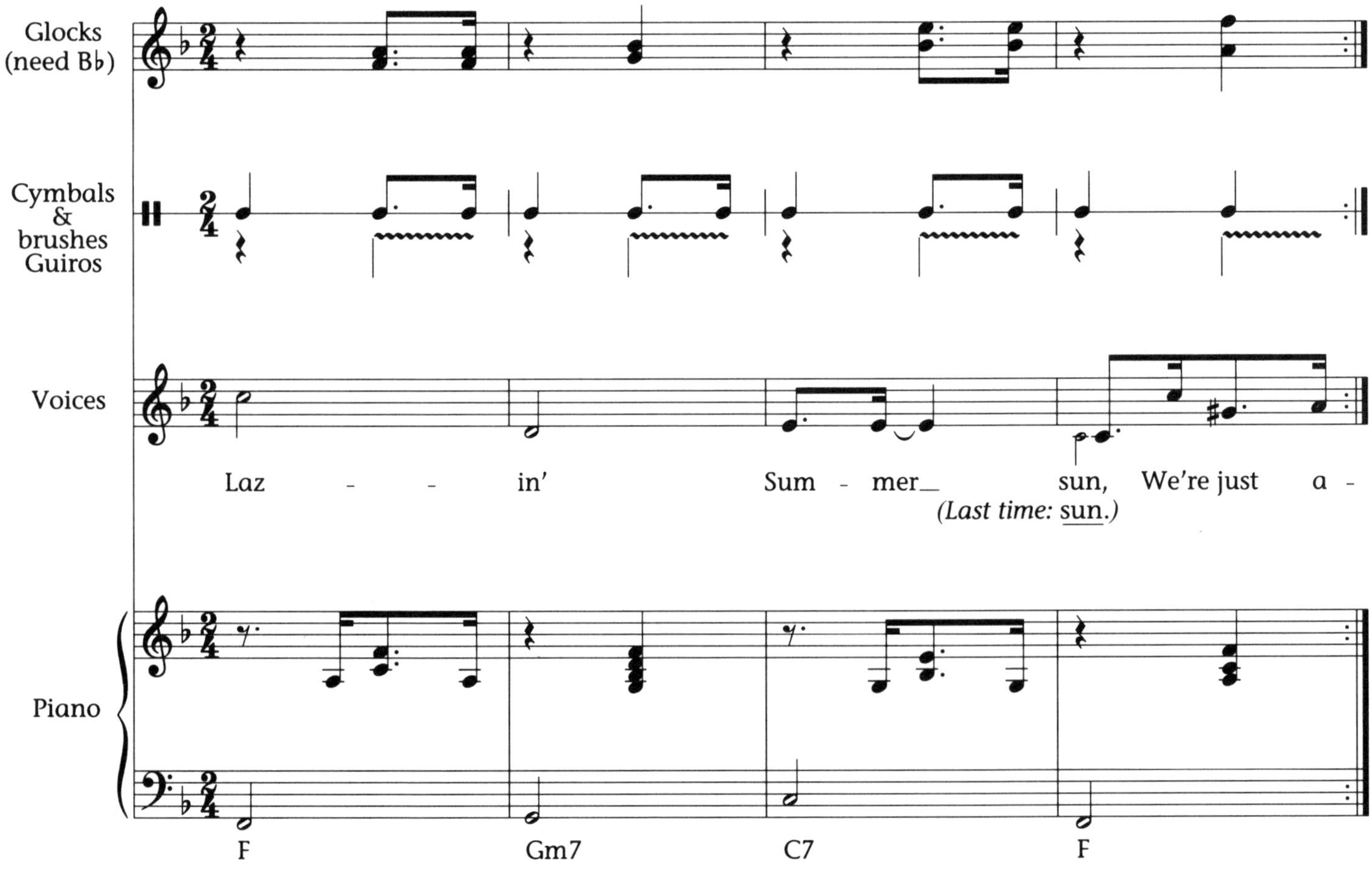

Glocks (need B♭)

Cymbals & brushes
Guiros

Voices

Laz - - - in' Sum - mer sun, We're just a -
(Last time: sun.)

Piano

F Gm7 C7 F

Autumn (2 part round)

Words and Music by
Eileen Diamond

Accompaniment Ostinato

The children may like to make-up and add an another instrumental part.
The round could also be used for infants if sung in unison as a short song.

Christmas (2 part round)

Words and Music by
Eileen Diamond

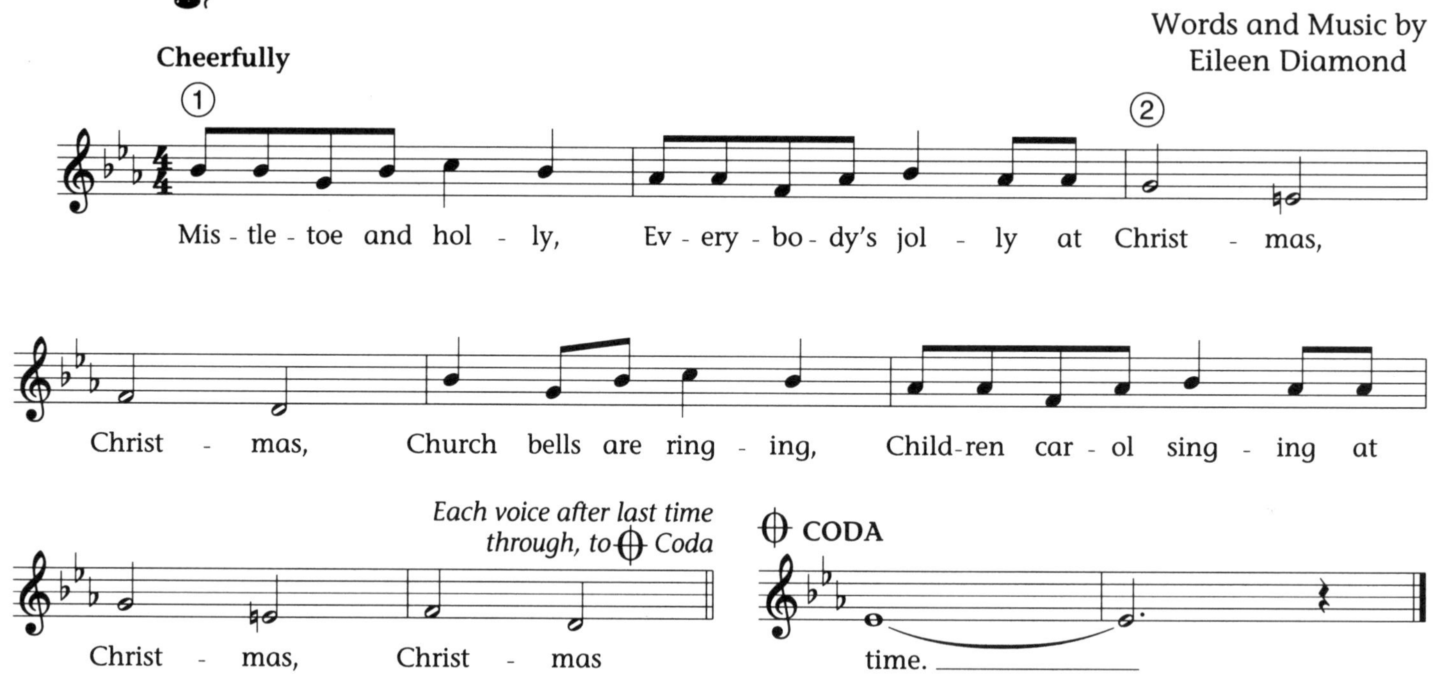

Accompaniment Ostinato

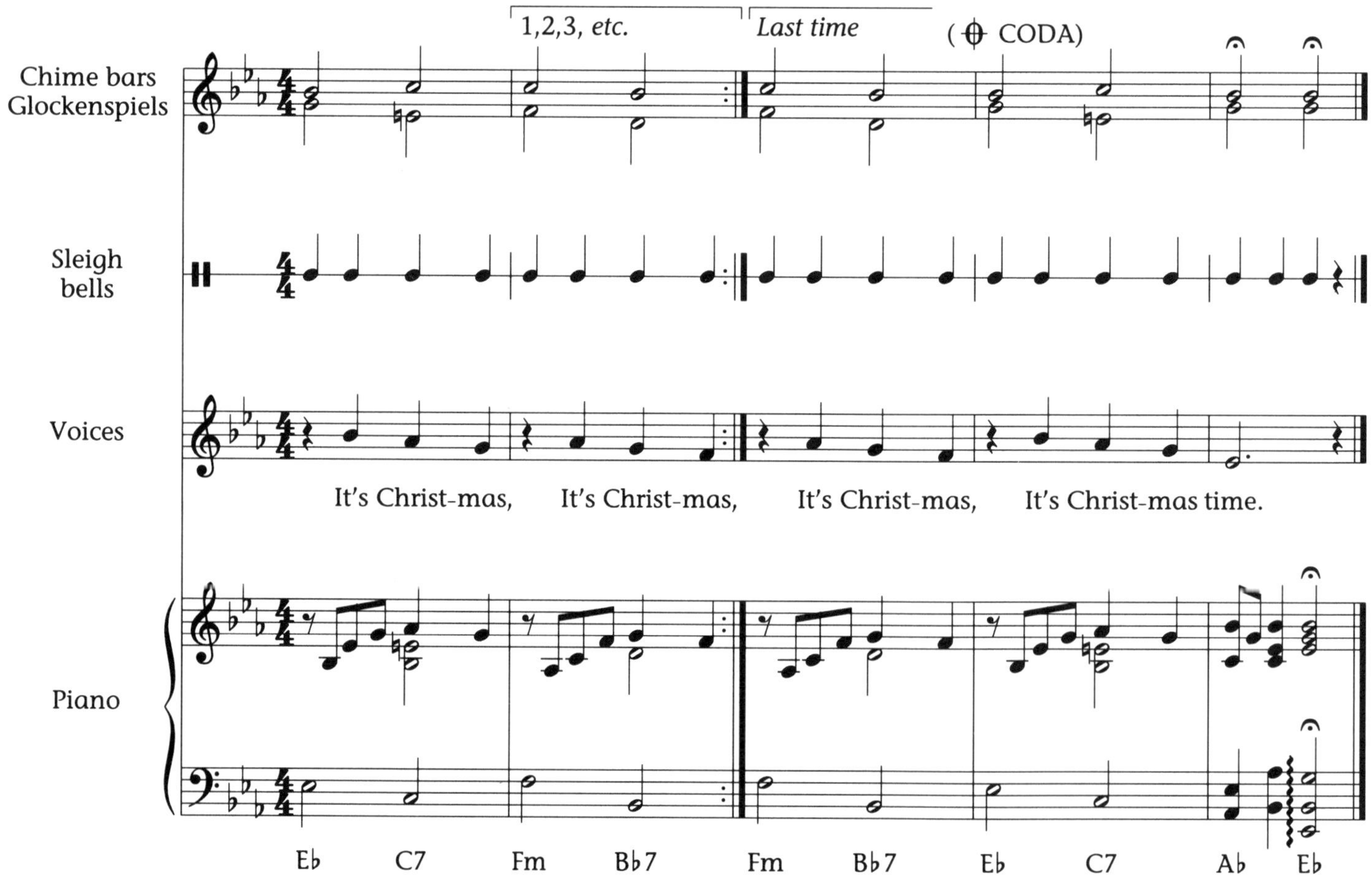

1,2,3, etc.

Last time

(CODA)

Chime bars
Glockenspiels

Sleigh
bells

Voices

It's Christ-mas, It's Christ-mas, It's Christ-mas, It's Christ-mas time.

Piano

Eb C7 Fm Bb7 Fm Bb7 Eb C7 Ab Eb

Going On A Journey

Words and Music by
Eileen Diamond

Steadily

VERSE

Go-ing on a jour-ney,

ritard. *a tempo*

Dm Gm7 A7 Dm

go-ing on a jour-ney, Which way would you choose? A

Gm C7 F D7

car or a plane? A bus or a train? Which one will you use?

Gm7 C7 F A7 Dm Gm6 A7 Dm C7

CHORUS
GROUP 1
We'd take a car, it's best by far, Yes, that's the way we'd
GROUP 2
Go by plane, That's the on - ly way to
GROUP 3
Hop on a bus, it's best for us, Yes, that's the way to
GROUP 4
Take a train, an ex - press train. That's the way to
F
B♭
C7
For repeat of CHORUS
To VERSE (𝄋)
Last time
trav - el.
go.
go.
trav - el.
go.
go.
trav - el.
go.
go.
trav - el.
go.
ritard.
F
F
A7sus
A7
F

Going on a journey,
Going on a journey,
Which way would you choose?
A car or a plane?
A bus or a train?
Which one will you use?

TEACHING IDEAS

A topical song on the theme of transport and travel. The verse is sung in unison followed by an accumulative type of chorus which builds up into four parts.

Performance

First divide the voices into four groups and teach each group its chorus.
Then perform in the following way:

All sing the verse, then group one sing the chorus twice.

All sing the verse, then group two sing their chorus twice (alone) and then twice joined by group one.

All sing the verse, then group three sing their chorus twice (alone), then twice joined by group two and both groups twice joined by group three.

The verse is sung a final time with group four leading in the chorus.

At the end the chorus may be repeated any number of times.

Further discussion and development ideas

The verse and the chorus alternate between the keys of D minor and F major. Ask the children to listen while you play the two key chords on the piano:
Ask them which one sounded sad (minor) and which one sounded happy (major). At subsequent lessons'

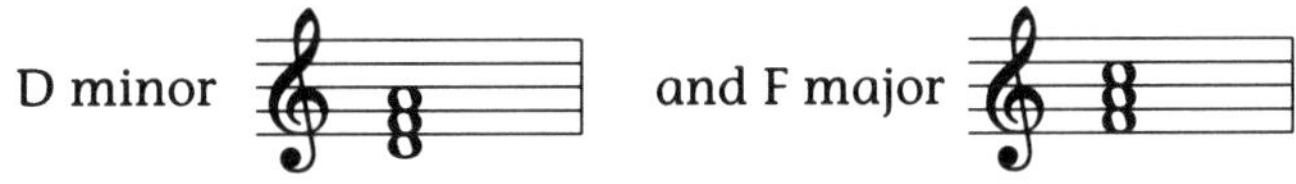

play one of the chords and ask the children to identify it as a major or minor.

Just For Him

Words and Music by
Eileen Diamond

1. Ma - ry and Jo - seph trav-elled by don - key, Then they found there was
2. Shep-herds ar - rived to wor-ship be - fore him, An - gels told them to
3. Choi - rs of an - gels sang of the splen - dour, Bells rang out on that
D7
Gm
C7
no-where to stay. An inn - kee-per told them he'd on - ly a sta - ble,
come from a - far. Three wise men came bear-ing gifts for the ba - by,
glor - i - ous morn. So on this day we will sing and re-mem - ber, The
F
F7
B♭
D.𝄋 Then last verse
to 𝄌 Coda
Where they could rest in the hay.
Gui - ded a - long by a star. Long a - day. Just for him
day that a ba - by was born.
C7
F
F♯°
F
F♯°
Gm7

CHORUS: Long ago far away in a manger,
A tiny baby slept in the hay.
Because of him we celebrate Christmas,
Just for him we remember this day.

1. Mary and Joseph travelled by donkey,
Then they found there was nowhere to stay.
An innkeeper told them he'd only a stable,
Where they could rest in the hay.

CHORUS

2. Shepherds arrived to worship before him,
Angels told them to come from afar.
Three wise men came bearing gifts for the baby,
Guided along by a star.

CHORUS

3. Choirs of angels sang of the splendour,
Bells rang out on that glorious morn.
So on this day we will sing and remember,
The day that a baby was born.

CHORUS (repeat last line.)

TEACHING IDEAS

This catchy Christmas song has a strong rhythmic feel which, after a little practice, should flow naturally. The instrumental accompaniment will provide a lift to the chorus.

Performance

INSTRUMENTS: XYLOPHONES, METALLOPHONES, CLAVES, SHAKERS.

When the song is known, practise the instrumental parts for the chorus separately. When they are secure put them together.

Xylophones and metallophones play the following pattern throughout the chorus: A - D - E - F

Starting on the third beat, they then play on the first and third beats throughout, until they reach the last three bars, when they should play on the first beats only. Be ready each time after the verse to start again on the third beat for the repeat of the chorus.

Claves and shakers each have their own rhythm to play throughout as follows:

Claves: 4/4 ♩. ♪ ♩ ♩

Shakers: 4/4 ♩ ♪ ♩ ♪ ♩

The Market Song

Words and Music by
Eileen Diamond

Cheerfully

One day when I went to the mar - - ket, I went to a col - our - ful stall, The own - er was there he was shout - ing his

F C7 F C7 F Bb G C7 F Fm6 C7 Gm C F

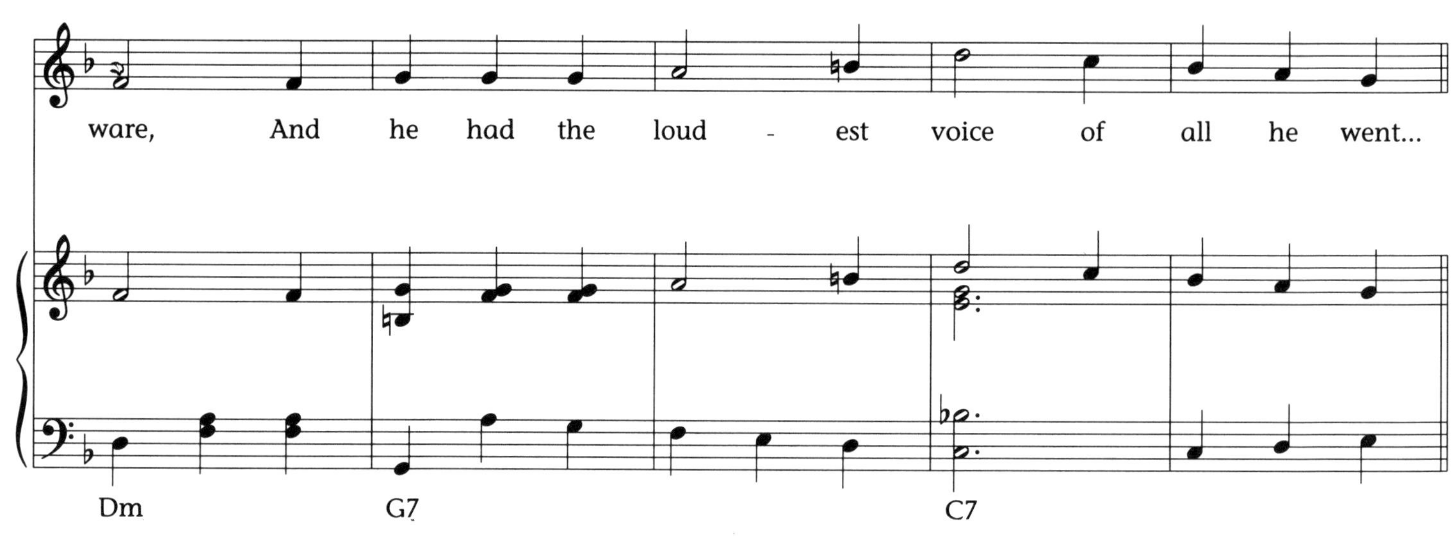

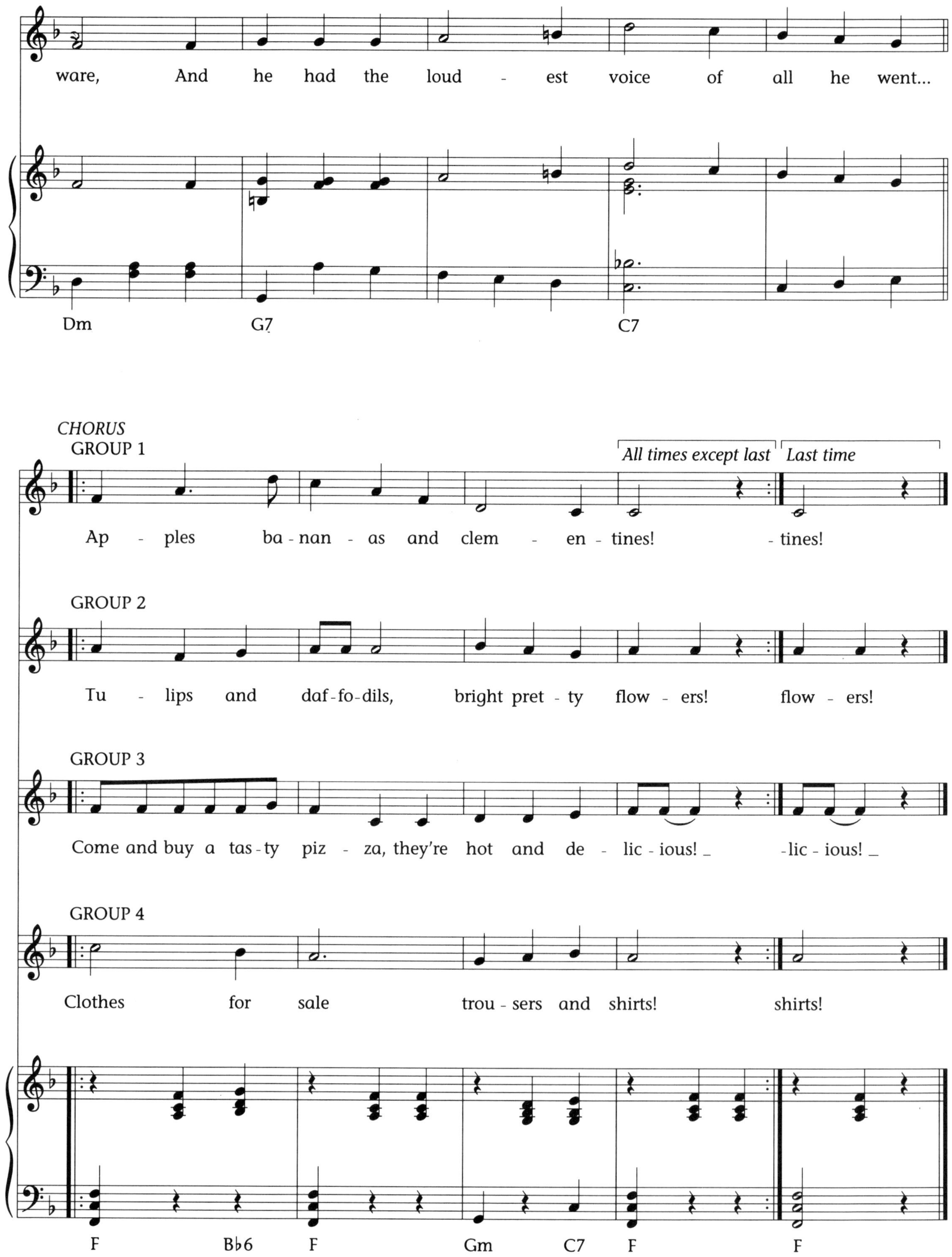

CHORUS

GROUP 1

All times except last *Last time*

Ap - ples ba - nan - as and clem - en - tines! - tines!

GROUP 2

Tu - lips and daf - fo - dils, bright pret - ty flow - ers! flow - ers!

GROUP 3

Come and buy a tas - ty piz - za, they're hot and de - lic - ious! _ - lic - ious! _

GROUP 4

Clothes for sale trou - sers and shirts! shirts!

F Bb6 F Gm C7 F F

One day when I went to the market,
I went to a colourful stall.
The owner was there
He was shouting his ware,
And he had the loudest voice of all he went . . .

TEACHING IDEAS

This song has a lilting verse sung in unison and a chorus which is accumulative and builds up into four parts. The children are introduced to controlling their own part within a group.

Performance

Divide the children into four groups for the chorus and teach each group their market call. These are short and easily learnt. The performance format is as follows:

All sing the verse, then group one sing their chorus twice through.
All sing the verse, then group two sing their chorus twice (alone) and then twice joined by group one.
All sing the verse, then group three sing their chorus twice (alone), then twice joined by group two and then both groups twice joined by group one.
The verse is sung a final time and group four lead in the chorus the other groups following in turn.

At the end the choruses may be repeated any number of times.

Further discussion and development ideas

For a concert performance set up some market stalls with the various groups standing behind them. The stall holders sing their calls and the visitors to the market sing the verse.
Introduce some topical links e.g. the origins of markets, market smells, and produce etc.
The children may like to make up some other market calls.

Sailing (3 part round)

Words and Music by
Eileen Diamond

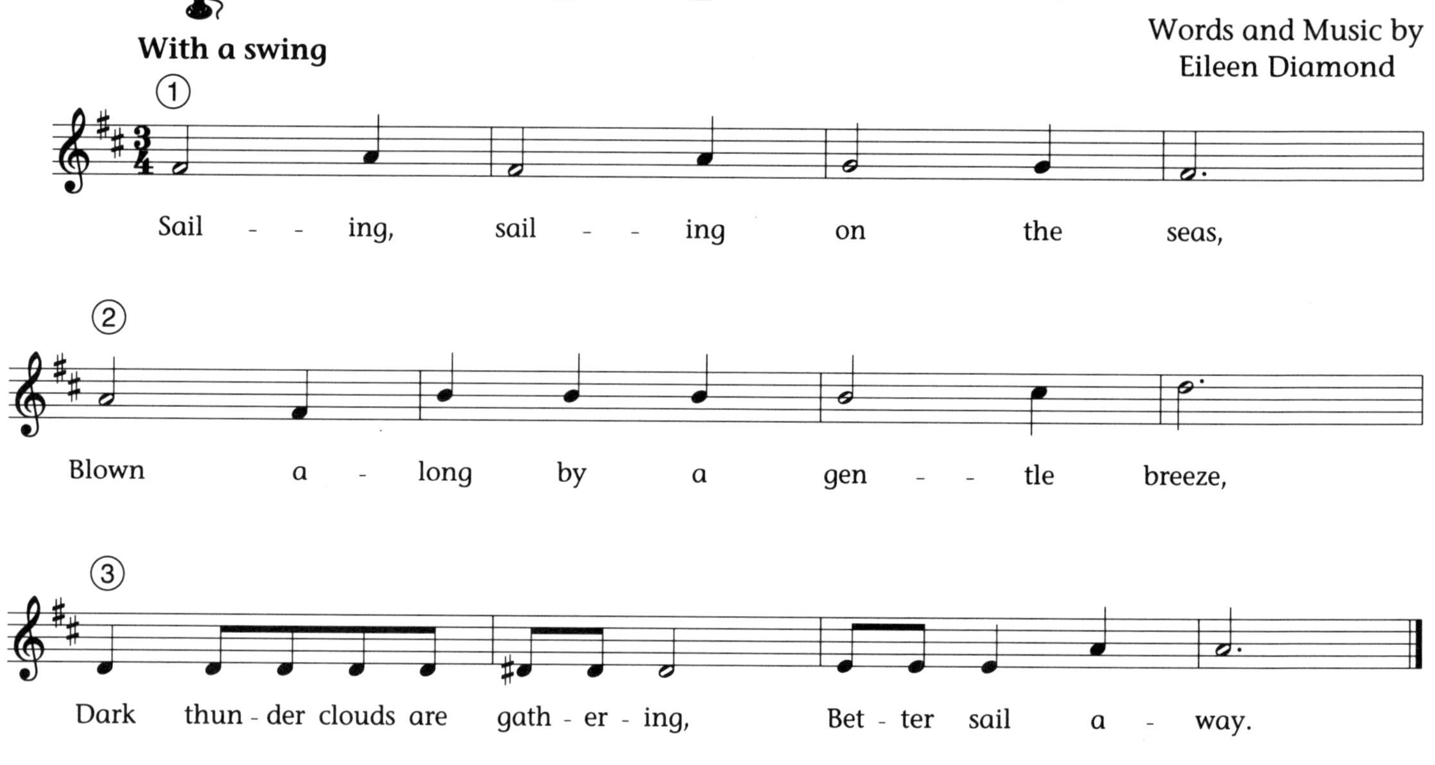

Accompaniment Ostinato

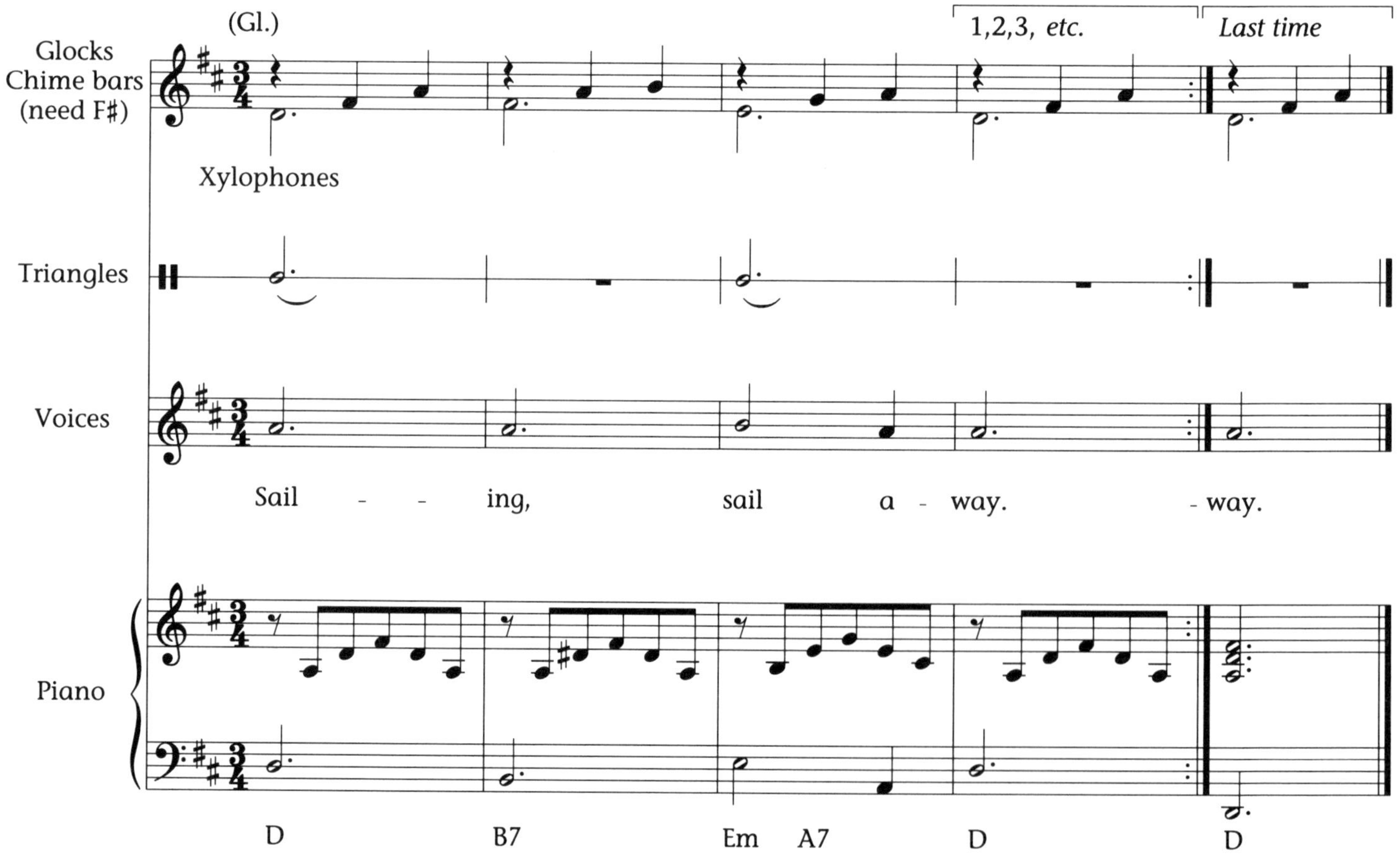

(Gl.)

1,2,3, *etc.* | *Last time*

Glocks Chime bars (need F♯)

Xylophones

Triangles

Voices

Sail - - ing, sail a - way. - way.

Piano

D B7 Em A7 D D

Sing Dance And Play

Words and Music by
Eileen Diamond

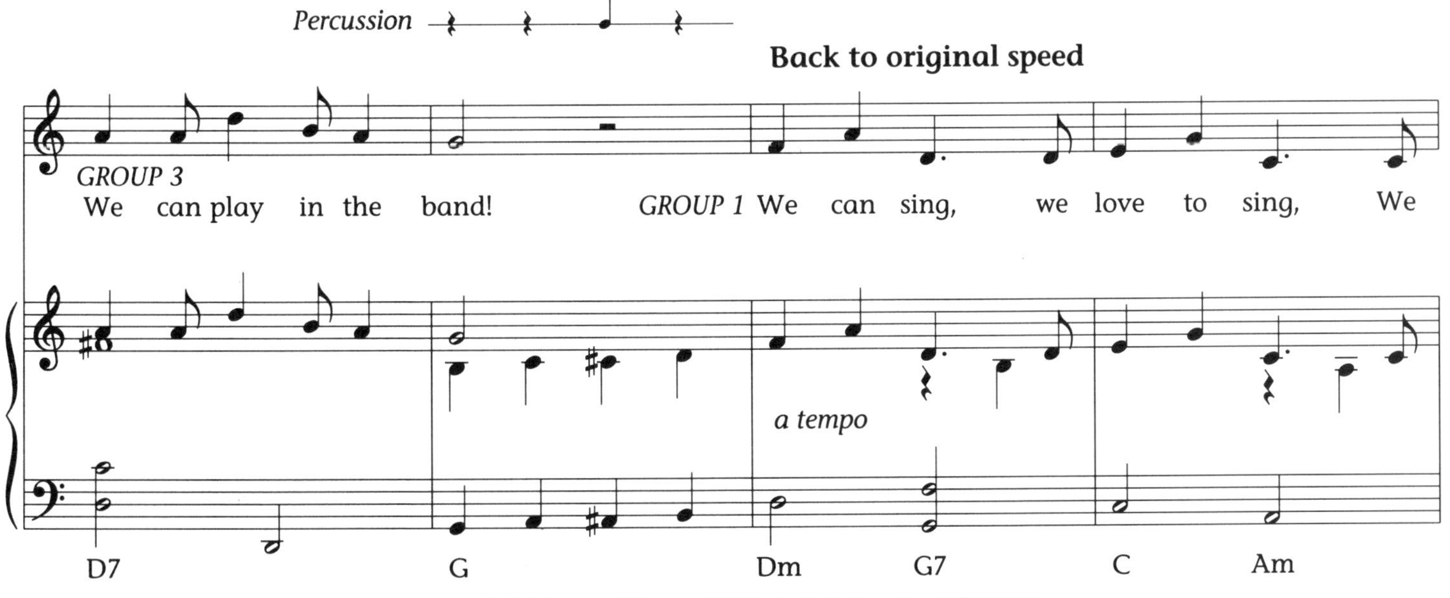

don't need words, we'll sing like hum-ming birds. Mm mm mm, mm, mm, mm,
Dm G7 C C#° Dm G7 C Am
mm mm mm. Group 2 We can dance, we love to dance,
D7 G F G7 C C#°
One, two, three, hop, one, two, three, hop. Hear the mu - sic,
Dm7 G7 C Dm Eb° C F G7
feel the beat, We've got rhy - thm in our dan - cing feet.
C A7 D7 G Em Eb°

Recorders
Xylophones/ Metallophones
Mixed Percussion
GROUP 3
We can play, we love to play At all e - vents, Just lis - ten to our in - stru- ments.
Dm G7 C Am Dm G7 C C#°
slower
GROUP 1 We can sing, la la la la. GROUP 2 We can
rit.
Dm G7 C Am Dm
Glocks & Xylos.
gliss.
Recorders
Glocks & Xylos.
Perc.
dance. Group 3 We can play.
G7 C Em Dm G7 C

ALL: Music is wonderful,
You can hear it throughout the land.

GROUP 1: We can sing!

GROUP2: We can dance!

GROUP 3: We can play in the band!

GROUP 1: We can sing, we love to sing
We don't need words,
We'll sing like humming birds.
Mm mm mm, mm mm mm, mm mm mm.

GROUP 2: We can dance, we love to dance,
One, two, three, hop, one, two, three, hop.
Hear the music, feel the beat,
We've got rhythm in our dancing feet.

GROUP 3: We can play, we love to play
At all events,
Just listen to our instruments.

GROUP 1: We can sing, la la la la.

GROUP 2: We can dance.

GROUP 3: We can play.

TEACHING IDEAS

A happy lively song encouraging different musical reactions.

Performance
Instruments:

TUNED PERCUSSION - RECORDERS, XYLOPHONES, METALLOPHONES/GLOCKENSPIELS.
UNTUNED PERCUSSION - DRUMS, TRIANGLES, TAMBOURINES, CLAVES/WOODBLOCKS, ONE PAIR OF CYMBALS.

Divide the children into three groups:

The singers
The dancers
The players

Dancers

At the words *We can dance* twirl around once and do the same again at the end of the song after group one have sung *Do, me, so, do.* While they sing their verse (after group one have finished humming) group two hold hands with a partner and dance the polka steps, then stand still when group three start to sing.

Players

Tuned parts are optional. Cymbals play only on the first beat of each bar, except at the end, where they play with the other percussion instruments as indicated.

Where Is Your Home? (3 part round)

2

Words and Music by
Eileen Diamond

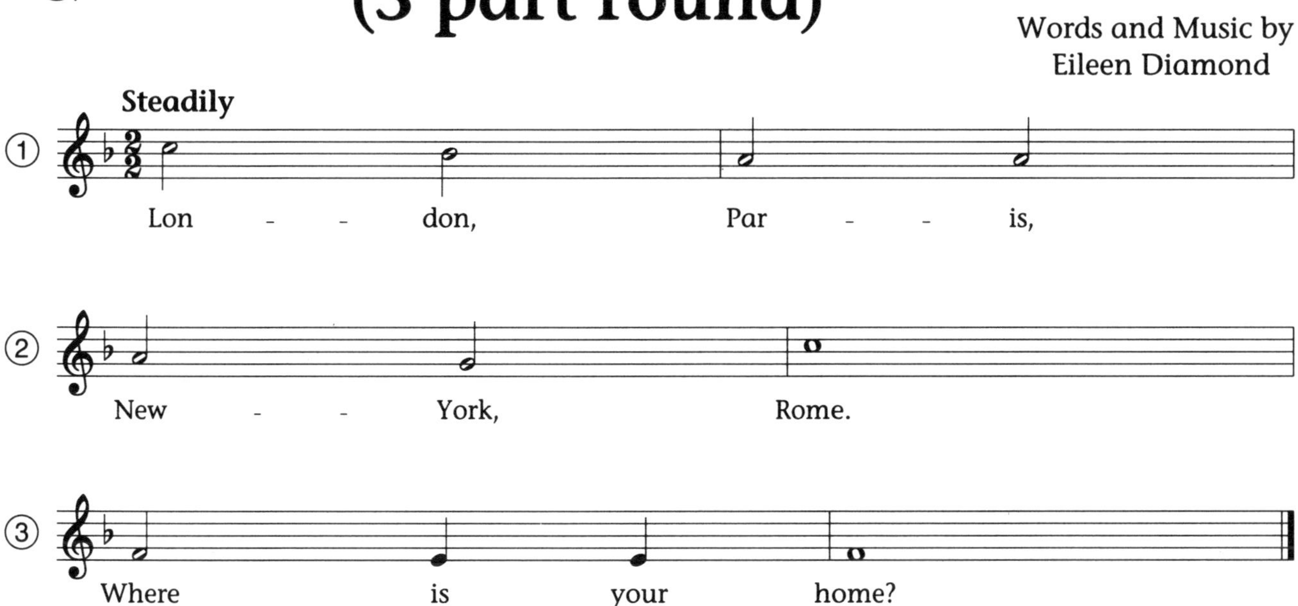

Accompaniment Ostinato

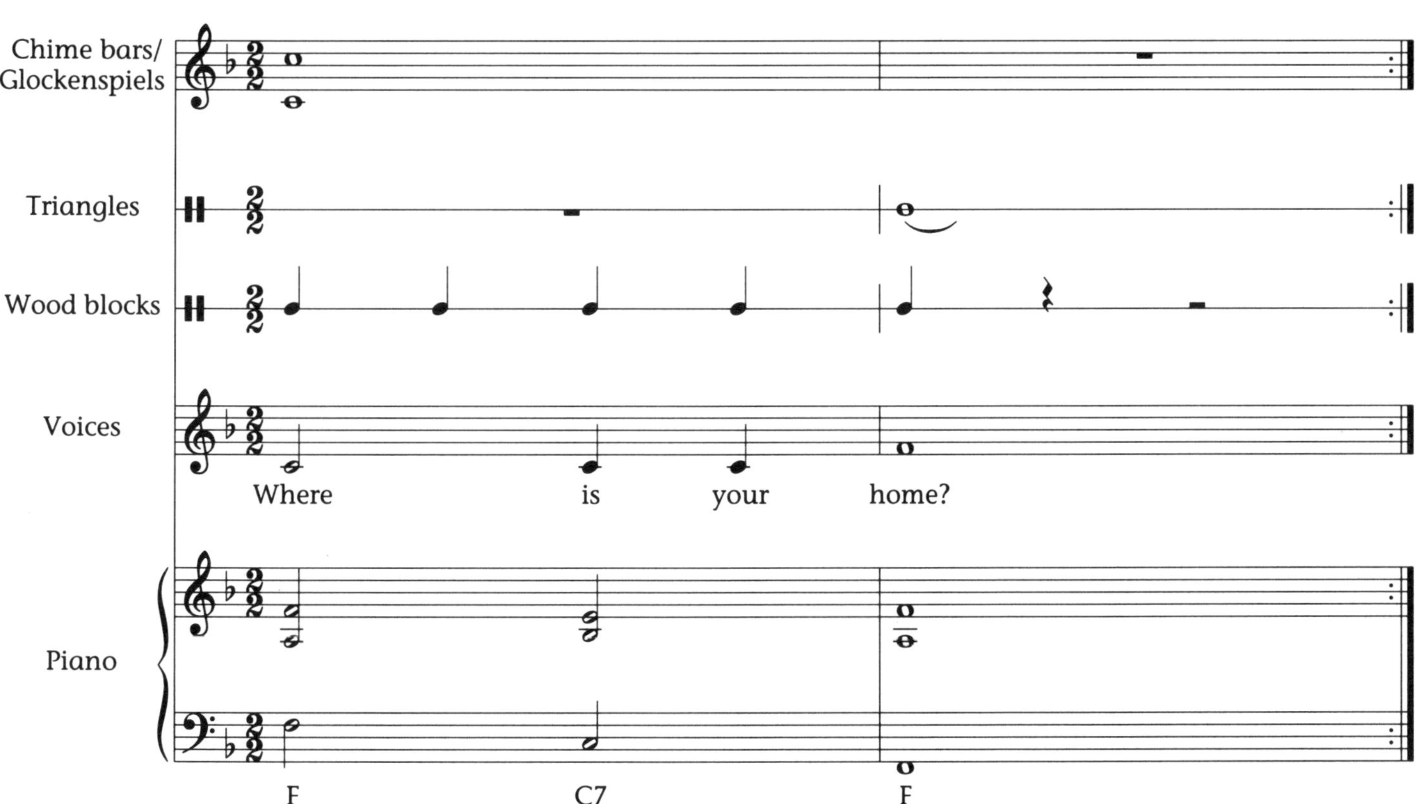

NOTE: Try varying the place names in the round — perhaps including some towns in your area. Ask the class to suggest different places, and encourage them to work out any new rhythms.

The Garage Round (4 part round)

Words and Music by
Eileen Diamond

Accompaniment Ostinato

The Crazy Round (3 part round)

Words and Music by
Eileen Diamond

Accompaniment Ostinato

Round starts on 3rd beat (2nd accomp. bar)